Through the Eyes of Santiago

The story of a Peruvian boy living an American maze

PEDRO A. SALAZAR

CAYMA PUBLISHING

First Edition: December 2018

ISBN: 978-1-7328923-1-6 (hardcover)
ISBN: 978-1-7328923-0-9 (paperback)
ISBN: 978-1-7328923-2-3 (ebook)

Library of Congress Control Number: 2018913897

Cayma Publishing, LLC.
Charlotte, North Carolina

caymabooks.com

Cover design by Diego Salazar

Photo by Sarah Miller Salazar

Printed in the United States of America

Events described are based on Mr. Salazar's memory of real word situations, including those shared by his brother with him. However, the names of all relatives, host families, and teachers—if given at all—have been changed. In addition, in each of the stories described, identifying details—such as age, gender, ethnicity, and nationality—have been modified. With one exception, the names of Mr. Salazar's friends have also been changed. Any resemblance to persons living or dead resulting from changes to names or identifying details is entirely coincidental or unintentional.

For:
Sarah Miller Salazar
Diego Salazar Bustíos
Carmela Bustíos Polar and family
Pedro Salazar Velarde and family
Mary Polar
Hermosina Velarde
Amy, Allen, and Harper Hendricks
Bill and Joyce Harper and family
Angela Jones and family
The Pisarik Family
The Hamilton Family
The Little Family
Alfredo and Nora Salazar
Mary Ellen Miller
Darrell and Susan Fisher
P. Manuel Cavanna Pertierra, S.J.
Rotary International

and "Blue Baby"

"My new world is white.
The clouds, the snow on the ground, even the people.
People speak to me and I don't understand.
All I can do is smile.
My new world is cold, unexpected, and utterly confusing.
My new world is Iowa."

Pedro A. Salazar

Introduction

THAT HIGH SCHOOL EXCHANGE STUDENT FROM PERU

This is the story of the year that changed the course of my life. We all have at least one experience that, for better or for worse, changed our lives. For some, it can be meeting "The One," having a child, or losing a loved one. For others, it may be learning a new language or discovering an exciting class in college. For me, it was the year I lived in the United States as an exchange student during high school.

It all began when my mother heard about the Rotary International Youth Exchange program, which provides an exceptional educational opportunity for high school students. Many of her friends' children had been part of it. The program required our family to host an exchange student in our home for one year, and in return, Rotary would send me abroad as an exchange student. My family discussed it and agreed that we were up for the challenge. Soon, my family was hosting Marie, an exchange student from France, for a year.

At first, it was strange to have a teenage girl living in our home. I was a sixteen-year-old Peruvian boy attending an all-male school. I had a brother, but no sisters, so I wasn't sure what to expect from Marie. She was a seventeen-year-old European girl who, before moving to Peru, had attended a co-ed high school. While Marie was fluent in English and French, she didn't know much Spanish, which was the spoken language in my home. Despite the initial culture shock—both for Marie and for us—it was an exciting experience. I was eager to learn about Marie and was constantly amused and intrigued by our cultural differences.

However, my excitement only lasted a few weeks. Between school and track and field practice, I had a full schedule. I didn't have much time to entertain my "sister." Complicating matters was the fact that she attended a different school, so I didn't see her during the day. When we were both at home, she would only ask me questions about Spanish vocabulary or grammar. I tried to help, but I didn't put forth the effort I should have. I was either too busy with my own homework or too tired after track practice.

With time, Marie successfully learned Spanish. She had a cute French accent that was easy to understand. As she became increasingly fluent in my language, I started to learn more about her as a person and what she thought of our culture and of us. In one of our conversations, she told me how hard it had been for her to even knock on my bedroom door to ask a simple question. She was very shy, nervous, unsure of herself, and uncomfortable about approaching anyone to ask for help.

Marie showed me a box she kept with several index cards in it, and she read a few of those cards to me. She didn't keep a diary; instead, she used those cards to write down her thoughts about her day or week. She wrote about her life in Peru in simple paragraphs, sometimes using just one word—the "Word of the Day," as she called it. In these cards, Marie always tried to put a positive spin on things, even when she was struggling.

It took me a while to understand why she had been scared to ask me for help and how difficult it must have been for her to leave her family and immerse herself in a new world. In fact, it took me a whole year to understand what she went through—a year of living in the United States, away from my family and friends, and immersed in another language.

When people ask me about my experience as a foreign exchange student, I usually only tell them about superficial details, the good times, and the funny anecdotes. I tell them about my first week in the United States and my initial culture shock. I tell them about the highlights of my "honeymoon" period. Every student goes through one. It's a period of excitement, a continuous high, when everything is new and different. Unfortunately, for most students, this period only lasts a few weeks. I was lucky: mine lasted much longer. Perhaps it was because I was experiencing extreme changes within my new environment. Or perhaps it was because I learned more than I had ever expected.

What I don't tell people is that the honeymoon period is only part of the experience. Although I felt loved and cared for throughout most of my time as an exchange student, I also experienced loneliness and deep sadness. I lived with loving families, but I often felt homesick. At one point, I was so frustrated that I considered leaving the exchange program and going home to Peru. Even though my friends and host families in the United States embraced me, I occasionally felt rejected by some Americans. And although most people accepted me, I also experienced racial discrimination for the first time in my life.

When I decided to spend a year as a high school exchange student in the United States in 2000, I did not expect that my time in Iowa would change the course of my life forever. After growing up surrounded by concrete structures in Arequipa, the second-largest city in Peru, I moved to Mount Vernon, a small Iowa town surrounded by cornfields. During my year there, I adapted to this new world, learned a new language, and made lifelong friendships. Most importantly, my year in the United States opened my eyes to a new world of possibilities. Four years later, my brother, Diego, embarked on a similar trip to Fort Dodge, Iowa. Diego's time in the Midwest also made a significant impact on his life. The Rotary International Youth Exchange program changed our lives in ways we never could have imagined.

This is why, about twenty years later, I decided to share my story. Marie's tale as an exchange student took the form of a box full of index cards. Mine is in this book. The main character of this book, Santiago, describes my life in Iowa, while also incorporating certain details from my brother's time in the Midwest.

This is the story of an exchange student who lived in the United States for a year. It's the story of two host families and of the many Americans who changed my life and had their lives changed by my time among them. It's the story of an immigrant, of a brown boy living in white America for the first time. And since I proudly chose to become a United States citizen later in life, it's also an American story.

Although I have a profound interest in politics, I don't have a political agenda. However, I do have a voice. It's a voice shaped by the struggles of growing up in Peru, a beautiful country with wonderful people, but also plagued by corruption and social injustice. Through my experiences and opinions, you will see the United States from the perspective of a young student from Peru. A Spanish-speaking immigrant. A dream-seeker eager to live his dream.

You will see the United States through the eyes of Santiago.

Chapter One
LEAVING LIMA

January 15, 2000

"Santiago, please bring a coat. It'll be cold on the plane," my mother said.

Her words didn't make much sense to me. It was the middle of summer in the Southern Hemisphere, and during the summer in Lima, Peru, the heat and humidity can be unbearable. Carrying a coat didn't seem like a good idea.

Most Peruvians didn't have internet access at home back in 2000, and Internet cafés had just started to appear in my hometown, so to learn about my intended destination, we had gone to my high school's library, which had very limited information about Iowa. We did find a book that described Iowa as an agricultural state, and it contained a couple of pictures. Based on these photos, which depicted Iowa during the summer months, it looked like a beautiful place. There was no indication that Iowa had harsh winters. As a result, the weather was the least of my concerns.

In fact, I was much more concerned about departing without any drug-related hiccups. At the time, Peru was a renowned exporter of marijuana and cocaine to the United States. In the weeks leading up to my trip, my mother had been constantly reminding me to be careful at the airport.

"You never know who might try to put drugs in your bags, Santiago," she said repeatedly.

Local drug lords had been using a system in which they would place drugs in the suitcases of unsuspecting victims and use them as "mules." Once the victim arrived in the United States, drug dealers would either steal the suitcase or threaten the victim to get access to the drugs. The Peruvian government had been airing dramatizations of the process on television in an effort to warn families about this strategy. Most of these dramatizations depicted a stranger placing a package in the bag of the perfect victim: a young, inexperienced and naïve traveler. Then, when the youngster tried to go through customs, airport officials would stop the victim and arrest them for attempting to smuggle drugs into the United States. As a result, I understood my mother's concerns and agreed to be careful with my luggage. After all, I was the perfect target: a seventeen-year-old boy traveling alone to the United States.

Not being from Peru's capital city, Lima had always been an enigma to me. It is a large, convoluted, dangerous, and disorganized city. Traffic is chaotic. Even one of its nicknames is unappealing: *La Fea*, meaning *The Ugly*. It got this undeserved nickname because apart from the sunny summer days, an unrelenting gray cloud covers it the rest of the year. Still, despite its problems, Lima is an interesting place to visit. It's a city with modern shopping malls standing beside historic ruins. A place where, to most *Limeños*, stop signs are merely a suggestion. A metropolis full of majestic churches surrounded by homeless people selling candy on the street. Lima is a beautiful mess.

"Santiago, please at least take this sweatshirt with you," my mother insisted once again.

"Okay, Mom. If it makes you feel better." I placed my hand on her left shoulder, and with a smirk, I added, "But just so you know, I don't think I'll need it." My mother smiled and walked toward her guestroom to pick up her purse.

I grabbed my blue sweatshirt, my backpack, and one of my suitcases and walked to the elevator down the hall, where my aunt, Ana, was waiting for me. She had already grabbed my other suitcase. I realized that it was a small elevator, and with my two suitcases, it was a tight fit. My mother would have to ride down separately.

Ana had moved from Arequipa, our hometown, to Lima a few years back. She and her husband owned a condo on the fourth floor of a building in San Borja, a suburb of Peru's capital city. Every time we visited Lima, my family stayed at her place, and this time was no different.

The elevator door closed, I took a deep breath, and Ana smiled at me. She noticed that I was not being myself. "Are you nervous?" she asked. I didn't know what to say. Although I did feel a little anxious, I wanted to give her the impression that I had everything under control.

"I hope my bags make it to Dallas okay, that's all," I responded. The tone of my voice gave me away and revealed that I was indeed nervous and a bit scared.

She attempted to calm my anxiety by reminding me of all the trips I had taken with my family as a child: "Don't worry, Santiago. You've traveled so much already. This is just another trip." I didn't think those trips were at all similar to my upcoming American adventure, but I could tell she was being nice and trying to make me feel better.

When I was a child, my parents made a point of regularly traveling with my extended family. We went to different cities in the southern region of Peru and in the northern part of Chile, especially during the summer months. I was also a member of the city of Arequipa's track and field team, which meant that I traveled to regional and national tournaments several times a year by bus. Those bus trips took me to Trujillo and Chiclayo in northern Peru, to Lima in central Peru, and to Tacna in the south. By the age of seventeen, I had traveled throughout most of coastal Peru and northern Chile. *I suppose she does have a point*, I thought.

When we reached the ground floor, we stepped out of the elevator and walked to Ana's car. Joaquin, my twelve-year-old brother, was already waiting in the back seat. He was happy to tag along to the airport as he loved planes. I placed my bags in the trunk of Ana's car and then climbed into the front passenger seat. A few moments later, my mother joined us and jumped into the back seat with Joaquin.

"Put your seatbelt on, please," Ana said seriously, as a reminder that most *Limeños* drove like NASCAR drivers. Plus, Ana had only recently obtained her driver's license, and her driving skills were still a little rusty. I buckled my seatbelt and made sure my mother and Joaquin did the same.

"This'll be fun," I whispered.

Our plan was to stop at *Restaurante Canchita*, Ana's favorite, for dinner on our way to the airport. Known for serving traditional Peruvian dishes, it rarely disappointed the demanding clientele of Miraflores, a wealthy neighborhood of Lima. Although Ana did not live in Miraflores, she frequented this neighborhood on weekends to try new restaurants and shop with her family.

We arrived at *Canchita* around six in the evening, and since my flight didn't board until 11:30 p.m., we had plenty of time to enjoy a relaxed meal. I ordered *lomo saltado*, a dish composed of small cuts of beef tenderloin, red onions, tomatoes, and Peruvian spices, with French fries and rice on the side. It is simple, but delicious. I wasn't all that hungry, but I knew I needed to eat something. The meal would be my last until I arrived in the United States, so I wanted to enjoy one last taste of Peru.

While we waited for our food to arrive, my mother once again ran through a list of items I may have forgotten to pack: "Did you pack your Walkman?"

"Yes, Mom."

"What about your sandals?"

"Of course."

"Your soccer cleats?"

"Yes."

"Your dictionary?"

I panicked. I wasn't sure if I had packed my Spanish-English dictionary. I reached for my backpack, and it was there. Thank goodness. If I wanted this year to be a great one, this dictionary would have to become my new best friend. I had to learn English quickly.

My mother leaned over and took the dictionary from my hands. She began to quiz me, asking me the meanings of a few simple English words. I attempted to answer her, but I got them wrong every time.

"Didn't you take English in school?" she asked, grinning.

I looked at her, half-smiling myself, and responded, "Yeah, something like that." We both laughed. English was the required foreign language in my high school's curriculum, so I had technically taken it. However, my school's English program didn't have a good reputation, and I was a prime example of this.

This wasn't our English teacher's fault. He was an excellent teacher who just happened to be tasked with an impossible job: teaching English to a group of uninterested students. And I was one of them. Even though I was a good student, I never applied myself in English class. I enjoyed learning about Spanish literature and Peruvian history, but I had no interest in learning the proper use of the verb "to be" in English. Most of my fellow students felt the same way.

However, after I found out that I would be traveling to the United States, I realized that I needed to polish my poor English skills. A few months before my trip, I bought a CD by the British band Oasis to help me learn English. Day after day, I tried to sing along to their songs with the help of the printed lyrics in the CD booklet, hoping this would help. Although I had good intentions, I soon realized that muttering song lyrics wasn't the most efficient way to learn proper English pronunciation and to expand my vocabulary.

My mother handed my dictionary back to me. As I searched for the words she had questioned me about, it once again became clear that I had plenty of work to do. Even though I wasn't sure exactly how much work was ahead of me, I knew I was in trouble.

Soon after, our meals arrived, and for a few minutes, my family took a break from laughing at my expense. It was time to eat.

Within our family, I was known for being the "slowest eater in the world," but on this occasion, I finished my meal before anyone else. I excused myself from the table and walked to the restroom to splash my face with cold water. I needed to freshen up and clear my mind.

Once in the bathroom, I saw my reflection in a mirror. I was scared. Although I had been preparing for this trip for months, now that it was time for me to leave my family, I was overwhelmed. I wanted to be part of the exchange program because I wanted to have a unique experience. I thought that by learning English and living in a different country, I would have a better chance of landing a good job in Peru in the future. At the same time, and although I am someone who welcomes change, I was afraid of the unfamiliar. What if this experience wasn't what I expected? What if my host family didn't like me? What if I didn't fit in?

After a few minutes of panic, I took a deep breath and splashed some cold water on my face to calm my nerves. "You've got this. It's okay," I muttered to myself as I left the bathroom and rejoined my family at our table.

* * *

"Let's go. Traffic picks up after eight p.m.," Ana eventually said after we had spent some time joking and talking in the restaurant. Her job was to get us to the airport on time, and I could tell she was nervous, too—not about my departure, but about driving through the chaos of Lima's streets.

Ana took the Costa Verde highway, which runs along Lima's shoreline. It's a popular route among tourists and has stunning views. With the Pacific Ocean on one side and a steep cliff jutting up beside us on the other, I observed, with a certain degree of national pride, the modern buildings that defined the Lima skyline at the top of the cliff. It was a beautiful summer night.

Like most teenagers, I was an idealist and believed that positive changes were possible. I often wondered why a country like Peru, which is filled with breathtaking landscapes, vast natural resources, complex biodiversity, delicious food, and wonderful people, had so many social and economic problems. I didn't know the answer, but I hoped my experience in the United States would help me find it. My hope was to better understand life in a developed country and learn a thing or two that I could take back home.

As we got closer to the airport, we stopped at a traffic light. A child approached my open window. He was probably eight or nine years old and was holding a box filled with bubble gum and candy. His worn-out sandals, tired eyes, and dirty clothes made it clear that he had been on the street for a while. He asked me if I wanted to buy a piece of gum. Although it broke my heart every time I saw a child working on the streets of Peru, this scene was familiar to me. Unfortunately, extreme poverty forced many Peruvian children to help their parents put food on the table.

"What's your name?" I asked.

"Juan," he answered in a sweet, shy voice.

"Where are your parents?"

He quickly pointed to the street corner, but no one was there. His automatic response seemed rehearsed. I had a feeling this wasn't the first time a stranger had asked him about his parents. I gave him some money but refused to take any candy. That was my usual response to such incidents. I didn't know whether it was the right thing to do, but I usually tried to help those kids in need in some way. He smiled and walked away.

"Those kids are everywhere. It's sad, but what can you do?" my aunt said.

As we drove away, I looked into the side-view mirror and noticed that Juan had moved on to his next "client." Unsurprisingly, during the last few minutes of our drive to the airport, I thought about Juan and all the injustices and economic disparities of my homeland.

A few minutes later, we arrived at the airport. "Alright guys, we're here," Ana announced. I could tell she was proud of herself: we had made it to the airport without a scratch.

The Jorge Chavez International Airport, like the rest of Lima, is a chaotic place. It's composed of one long building, several counters, and long lines of passengers facing each counter. Peru had been trying to improve its main international airport for a few years, but it still had a long way to go.

As we walked toward the counters, I realized it was time to say goodbye to my relatives, which wasn't easy. Although I normally resorted to humor during such situations, this time, I kept the jokes to myself. I hugged Ana and gave Joaquin a kiss on the cheek. His watery eyes made it even more difficult to say *Adios*. It was a sad goodbye.

My mother and I walked to the counter together. Since I was underage, she had to check me in with the airport officials. I said a polite hello to the official at our counter, but she barely acknowledged me. She grabbed my passport, and the interrogation began: "Did you pack your own bags?"

"Yes, I did."

"Are you bringing any illegal substances or drugs of any sort?"

"No."

"Why are you traveling to the United States?"

"To be an exchange student."

"Do you have family there?"

"Yes, I have relatives in New York City."

Her questions continued without a pause. They all seemed too long, too detailed, and too excessive, but I answered all of them. When they finally ended, she stared at me for a few seconds. Feeling cheeky, I added, "I have a dog, too, and I'm not dating anyone." I smiled, but the airport official didn't seem to share my sense of humor.

"You know, I've been sitting here for twelve hours, and I'm tired of dealing with comedians like you," she said, shaking her head.

Perfect. With a single silly comment, I had managed to upset an airport official. I didn't know what to say, but I knew I had to apologize. Immediately. "I'm so sorry," I said as I began to shake with fear. I started sweating, and my heart was pounding hard.

The official placed my passport on the counter, grabbed her pen, and pointed it at me. "Kid, you're too gullible. You're fine. I actually thought your joke was funny," she said with a smirk. The joke was on me. It was all part of some sort of dark airport humor. "Have a good trip," she added and handed me my passport.

With that, it was time to say goodbye to my mother. "Okay, this is where I have to leave," I said as we walked toward the security checkpoint together.

She smiled. "You'll be fine, Santiago. Just don't forget to let me know when you arrive in Iowa."

I gave her a tight hug and a kiss on the cheek. She wasn't smiling anymore, and I noticed some tears starting to escape her eyes. "Mom, we'll see each other again in no time. It's only a year," I said, trying to reassure her. She nodded, so I shouldered my backpack and got in line with the other passengers at the security checkpoint. She couldn't come any further with me, so I waved a last goodbye.

Just as I went through security, I heard my mother shouting, "Santiago, your sweatshirt! You forgot your sweatshirt!" A security guard grabbed the sweatshirt from her and handed it to me. I smiled and thanked him.

"Oh, Mom," I whispered, rolling my eyes.

Chapter Two
SALT

January 16, 2000

My plane landed at the Dallas/Forth Worth International Airport without any problems. Compared to the Lima airport—and to any airport I had ever been to in Peru, for that matter—the airport was clean and well organized. Also, it was a great place for me to arrive, as most signs were in both English and Spanish. I picked up my suitcases, went through customs and immigration, and searched for my next gate. Annoyingly, my next gate was in a different terminal, and since I didn't realize I was supposed to check my bags for my next flight at a counter close to the customs and immigration area, I ended up lugging my two big suitcases around the airport all the way to my gate.

Even though I was exhausted from the overnight flight and concerned about the prospect of taking a train to a different terminal, I was excited. I had always been fascinated by American life and culture, which I had previously only been able to see on cable TV, movies, and CNN *en Español.* So, when I was finally surrounded by Americans speaking to each other in English, a huge smile appeared on my face.

The temperature in Dallas was in the low seventies, and most of the men were wearing short-sleeved shirts and shorts. There were no traces of big coats, sweaters, or snow boots. I was wearing a sweatshirt, and I started to sweat from hauling my suitcases around. I again found myself questioning my mother's request that I wear a sweatshirt on my trip.

As I approached a food court to grab something to eat, I noticed the signs of many popular fast food restaurants. "McDonald's at the airport?" I whispered. I couldn't believe it. "Pizza Hut, too?"

My hometown of Arequipa, a city with a million people, didn't have American fast food chains. There was no McDonald's, no Pizza Hut, no Subway. Lima had a few fast food restaurants, but my family didn't visit the capital often, and even when we did, we didn't frequent those "classy" food hubs because they were on the expensive side. My family rarely ate out in general, and I grew up eating at home or at my grandparents' house. When we did go out, we usually visited traditional Peruvian restaurants.

I walked over to the Pizza Hut counter and examined the menu. After I decided what I wanted, I approached the cashier. I wasn't fluent in English, but I knew my numbers. "Number one, please," I said with a strong Spanish accent and handed him some money.

He asked me a question, but I didn't understand it, so I remained silent, giving him a blank stare. The cashier then handed me a receipt and, using hand gestures, directed me to the far end of the counter so he could help the next customer. I walked over to the soda station, filled my drink cup, and waited for my food.

A few moments later, a girl behind the counter said a few words, including, "Number one," as she placed a small pizza box on the counter. I grabbed it and walked away, already looking for an open table. Once I sat down, it didn't take me long to devour the pepperoni and cheese treat. This was my first American meal, and it was the beginning of my love/hate relationship with American fast food.

*   *   *

When I reached the gate for my flight to Iowa, I noticed that the scenery had changed. There were no more short-sleeved shirts and shorts. Instead, everyone was dressed in long-sleeved shirts and pants. Almost everyone had a jacket or coat of some kind. Also, nearly everyone was white.

Since I still had a few hours until my departure, I pulled out my newly purchased Walkman cassette player from my fanny pack and started listening to one of my Mar de Copas cassettes. Mar de Copas, a band formed in Lima in 1992, is my favorite Peruvian rock band, and their music is the soundtrack of my high school years.

Eventually, the lady at the United Airlines counter beside our gate began to call passengers to board. As I usually did in Peru when officers called passengers to board, I approached the counter and gave her my ticket. She grabbed it, shook her head, and gave it back to me. I did not know what to say, so I stepped aside. She did, however, notice my bags and asked me to hand them to her.

I noticed that only a few people were being allowed to board at this point. The lady kept calling passengers to board, but I wasn't sure when I would be allowed to do so. I only assumed it was safe to approach her again when most of the people in the departure lounge began to form a line at the gate. I rushed to the counter once again and gave her my ticket. Although I had noticed that other passengers were forming a line without approaching the counter, I thought I had to give my ticket and documents to the officer before boarding the plane, as was customary in Peru at the time. She spoke to me, but I didn't understand what she was saying. I shook my head in confusion, and she pointed at the line of passengers who were boarding the plane. I followed them.

I had only been in the United States for a few hours, and the language barrier had already become a problem.

Once onboard, I noticed that the airplane was surprisingly small, but I didn't think much of it. I had a window seat, and for a while, no one sat next to me. Unfortunately, just when I thought I would have the two seats all to myself, a large man walked into the cabin and looked directly at my row. I was not concerned about him sitting next to me; I was worried that he would try to start a conversation.

As he settled down beside me, I noticed that he wore a polo shirt, khaki pants, and white tennis shoes. He also carried a heavy winter coat. He had a large frame, so his arms encroached onto my seat. Even his hands and fingers were massive. He looked at me and, with a deep voice similar to that of a radio host, said hello. I responded in kind, hoping he would leave me alone after that, but he didn't. He pointed at my clothes and laughed, leaving me confused and inexplicably embarrassed. The man kept talking to me after that, but I didn't understand him, so I turned my head to the window and closed my eyes. He seemed ready to have a long conversation with me and wasn't catching on that I couldn't speak English. *What does he want?* I wondered. Fortunately, after several attempts to communicate with me, he gave up, mumbled a few words, and fell asleep.

As soon as he was asleep, I opened my backpack and grabbed my dictionary. I had a lot of work to do. "Hi, how are you? My name is Santiago, and you?" I said quietly in English. My dictionary included a few basic phrases that I clearly needed to learn before arriving in Iowa. But then what? What was I going to do when my host family wanted to talk to me and all I could say was, "I don't speak English," or "Slow down, please"? An uncomfortable feeling of anxiety began to settle in my mind as I looked out the window, seeking some comfort.

It was a lovely January day without a cloud in the sky. On the ground far below, I saw what appeared to be acres of green farmland. Fingering my sweatshirt, I smiled. I didn't know why my mother had worried about my being cold. The weather was beautiful.

I found some comfort in the scenery, but I couldn't keep my eyes open. I was tired and soon fell asleep. I woke to the sound of the pilot saying something I didn't understand over the plane's intercom, and soon after, we began our descent. I looked out the window again, excited to catch my first glimpse of Iowa. What I saw shocked me: the ground was no longer green, but rather a stark white. I rubbed my eyes and drank some water before taking another look. Whiteness everywhere. *How can this be? Where am I, the North Pole?* I wondered. Although I was concerned about the change in scenery, I couldn't help but admire the white landscape.

As we got closer to the airport, I realized that I might be in trouble. As we continued our descent, I noticed that most of the people around me had grabbed their coats. A lady across the aisle took a small winter coat from her backpack and put it on her child. The guy sitting next to me gave me one last strange look, raised his eyebrows, and pointed to his coat, which he was now wearing. Clearly, I wasn't prepared for what was coming. I grabbed my sweatshirt and put it on. I no longer questioned my mother's advice, and I was thankful that I had listened to her.

I looked through the window one more time. *I hope that's salt*, I thought.

Chapter Three
DEER HEADS, AMMO, AND DREAMCATCHERS

January 16, 2000

The crew opened the airplane's door, and cold air immediately rushed in. The passengers around me stood and began making their way to the exit. When my turn came, I grabbed my backpack, walked to the airplane door, and headed down the stairs that led outside. The airport didn't have jetways.

As I stepped out of the plane, I took a deep breath. It was one of those breaths that seem to instantly freeze you down to your bones. It was thirty degrees Fahrenheit in Cedar Rapids. The cold shocked me, as I had never experienced such extreme low temperatures before. I would soon learn that for a January day in Iowa, this was actually fairly mild. For now, I rubbed my hands together and blew some warm air into them. I didn't have winter gloves, and my sweatshirt wasn't much help against the cold.

Once I made my way to the gate inside, I spotted a group of people holding a Peruvian flag, and I waved to them. My host mom, Carrie Novak, smiled, approached me, and gave me a warm hug. She immediately made me feel welcome.

The guy holding the Peruvian flag was her son James— one of my host brothers. Clark, my other host brother, wasn't there, as he was away attending college. James was a couple of years older than me and fairly tall. He came forward next, and as I shook his hand, he said, *"Hola, cómo estás, hermano?"*

His perfect Spanish took me by surprise. *"Hola,"* I said in response.

My host dad, Edward Novak, approached me, shook my hand, said, "Hey, Santiago," and gave me a big hug. I couldn't stop smiling.

Finally, the two girls came up. Heather was about my age, and I gave her a kiss on the cheek. Macy, my youngest host sister, was about thirteen years old, and I also gave her a kiss. Both girls seemed taken aback by my salutation, but I didn't think much of it at the time.

We walked to the baggage claim area together to pick up my suitcases. The Cedar Rapids airport was smaller than any airport I had ever visited before, even in Peru.

James, still speaking perfect Spanish, asked me about my trip. I told him that everything seemed great so far. Curious, I asked, "Where did you learn to speak Spanish?" I was truly impressed with his grasp of the language.

"In Lima, Peru," he said. "I was a Rotary exchange student, just like you."

James translated some of our conversation for my host family as we waited for my bags. They all seemed interested to learn more about me, but it was difficult due to the language barrier.

It took a while, but the bags from my plane finally started to appear on the conveyor belt. When my two bags came out, I pointed them out. James grabbed one, Edward grabbed the other, and off we went, back out into the cold.

The Novaks had come to pick me up in two vehicles, due to our numbers. James invited me to ride with him in his red convertible. He explained that he didn't usually drive it in the winter, but it hadn't snowed for a few days, so the roads were clean.

"No snow in a few days?" I asked sarcastically, looking around at the snow-covered landscape.

James smiled. "Welcome to winter in Iowa, Santiago."

As we drove, he turned on the radio, and the song "Breathe" by Faith Hill came on. I found myself thinking, *The first song I hear in the United States is a country song. How fitting.* We drove along a highway for a few minutes, but then turned off onto a gravel road. After that, we were surrounded by miles and miles of farmland covered by snow. It was a sunny and windy day, and I couldn't understand how it could be cold outside when there wasn't a cloud in the sky.

During the winter, my hometown of Arequipa never gets snow. The temperature does drop, but the city never freezes. In fact, back home, the sun usually warms the town throughout the day, and the temperature rises to seventy degrees Fahrenheit by the afternoon. During the summer months, it is very rainy. Dark clouds cover the sky, and heavy rain falls almost daily. On most mornings, the clouds do break for a while, the sun shines for a few precious hours, and the iconic volcano, El Misti, comes into view again. The very top of the mountain is covered with snow only during those summer months. It is unreachable, majestic, and a beautiful sight for everyone to enjoy. The snow never falls on the city, though.

In Peru, when people talk about the United States, most talk about places like Miami, Los Angeles, and New York—

all crowded cities filled with skyscrapers. From what I could see, Iowa wasn't like that at all. The tallest buildings I had seen thus far were the airport tower and all the silos we drove past on our way to my host parents' home.

"What do they keep in those?" I asked, still speaking in Spanish, pointing at some silos.

"Corn."

"That much corn?"

"We have a lot of corn," he said with a smile.

James drove along the gravel roads much faster than I would have. I was wearing a seatbelt, but every time we made a turn, our car veered dangerously close to the edge of the road. It made me nervous.

"So, where is the house?" I asked.

"We're getting close. We live on a farm outside of Mount Vernon."

"Is Mount Vernon a city?"

"Not exactly. It's a small town. Iowa is full of them. We have more small towns than cities, honestly."

After passing a few more silos and some barns, we finally made it to the house. My host parents were already there. James and I parked in the driveway, which was part-gravel and part-concrete. I stepped out of the car, and a couple of peacocks wandered over to welcome me. I had only ever seen peacocks in books and was surprised to find them roaming around the driveway in the cold. A friendly dog ran toward me and licked my hand as I reached out to pet him.

The house had grey siding and a white door. A thin layer of snow covered the roof. A window just beside the door still displayed some Christmas lights. Although it was the middle of January, they hadn't taken down all of the Christmas decorations yet. I walked inside and was relieved to find that it was warm. The living room had a beautiful wood-burning fireplace, which provided the room with some warmth.

My host dad had already picked up pizza from a gas station nearby, and three pizza boxes now waited for us on the dinner table. Carrie handed me a plate, and I grabbed a slice of pizza and sat down at the table. I looked around for a fork and a knife, but I couldn't find them in plain sight. Surprisingly, no one else followed my lead. Instead, James, still speaking Spanish, asked me to join the family in the living room. There, they all sat on the couch or the floor while a movie played on the television in the background. I noticed that no one had grabbed utensils. They all ate their pizza with their hands, and although it seemed odd, I followed their lead.

In Peru, my maternal grandfather had taught me that one should always use silverware to eat. In America, most people don't follow that rule for things like pizza, wings, and appetizers. Here, finger food is a thing.

Although my host family clearly wanted to ask me about my trip and about myself, it was difficult to have a conversation. James translated for us, but it wasn't a fluid back-and-forth conversation.

After the movie that had been playing in the background ended, James grabbed his coat, said goodbye to the family, and left. He had already told me that he lived in the family's cabin on the Cedar River, which was just down the road. He had moved into the cabin a few months ago, as, being an adult, he enjoyed being close to the river and having a little more freedom and privacy. As a result, his former room in the farmhouse was now my room.

Soon after James left, Carrie, my host mom, showed me to my room. "Thank you," I said with a strong Spanish accent.

Carrie smiled. "Good night, Santiago."

I walked into my room and turned the lights on. Two deer heads mounted on the walls stared down at me. I had never been hunting in my life, and now I would be staying in a room that contained two dead animals. "Poor Bambi," I muttered.

When I was able to tear my eyes away from the deer heads, I saw that the room also contained a wooden dresser, a freestanding wooden wardrobe, a narrow bed, and a small nightstand.

In contrast, my room back home in Peru had a double bed, a spacious handmade wooden wardrobe, a wooden nightstand, a modern metal desk where I did my homework, and a small bookcase. The walls were covered with posters of surfers and skateboarders. A guitar, a pair of rollerblades, and a few pairs of athletic shoes completed the look. It was the room of a middle-class Peruvian city boy. I missed it already.

I started to unpack my clothes from my suitcase, but when I opened the wooden wardrobe, I realized that it was full of hunting rifles. Turning to the wooden dresser, I found that the top drawer was full of ammo. My room contained the heads of dead animals and the guns that had killed them. This wasn't my idea of a welcoming room. I raised my eyebrows, looked at one of the deer heads, and jokingly thought, *I hope my head doesn't end up on the wall as well.*

I opened another drawer in the dresser and found a hunting tee shirt, which I replaced with some of my clothes. The bottom drawer was empty, so I filled it with my athletic clothing and underwear. My jeans and sweatshirts would have to wait until I could ask Carrie or Edward where to move the ammo and rifles to make room for my clothes.

It had been a long day, and I was tired. I grabbed my toothbrush and walked to the bathroom. There were two bathrooms in the house: one for the "kids" and another for the parents. This meant that I would be sharing a bathroom with two girls. Two teenage girls. That would take some getting used to.

I brushed my teeth and returned to my room. I noticed that everyone else had already gone to sleep. I put on my pajamas, said a short prayer, and turned off the light. Instantly, the walls and ceiling lit up with glow-in-the-dark fluorescent stars. I had never seen anything like it.

I turned the lights back on to look for those stars up close. Instead, a strange object hanging by the nightstand next to a cross immediately caught my attention. It was a circle with a web or net inside of it. Feathers and beads hung from it. Was this some sort of witchcraft? I hoped not.

As I examined that strange object, I noticed a book on the nightstand below it. Its cover had a picture of the object. The title was *Dreamcatchers*.

Confused and somewhat concerned about all the items in my room, I turned the lights off once more. The "sky" lit up again. I took a deep breath and closed my eyes.

"Enough for day one," I whispered. It was time to sleep.

Chapter Four
BOY MEETS GIRL

January 17, 2000

I woke at six the next morning. My bed was warm, and leaving its coziness didn't seem appealing. After snoozing for a few minutes, I mustered the courage to face the cold and walked out of my room.

Carrie, who had been up for a while, welcomed me into the kitchen and grabbed a few boxes of cereal from the pantry. She put the boxes on the kitchen table, took a container of milk out of the refrigerator, and handed me a bowl. I poured some cereal and milk for myself, wondering, *Where is the maid, the cleaning lady, the cook?* Although I couldn't ask Carrie about them due to the language barrier, I had already noticed that the Novaks didn't have a live-in maid. *Perhaps they come later when everyone leaves for the day*, I thought.

Most middle-class families in Peru have a maid, and some have a maid and a cook. My family had a maid who cooked, which was the best of both worlds. She was around fifty years old and had been with our family for about ten years. She lived in a room my parents had built on the flat roof of our house, which we called the "third floor." When I tell Americans that I grew up with a live-in maid, many automatically assume that we had money. Of course, many

30

Peruvians who have maids are wealthy, but that is not the case for most families. It was not the case for mine. The truth is that having a maid or bringing in outside help is not nearly as expensive in Peru as it is in the United States. This is because Peru is still a country with a significant portion of its population living in extreme poverty.

When I was growing up, many of the maids who worked for urban middle-class families like mine came from areas where extreme poverty is prevalent: poor small towns high in the Andes. For those living in such harsh conditions, working as a live-in maid in the city is a way for them to have a warm meal every day, a roof over their head, some money to send back home, and an opportunity to live in a big city—or at least a town bigger than where they came from. Also, many of the maids arrived in the city as children and were raised by the families they helped. In a recent conversation, my mother explained that, many times, people in the Peruvian middle class would ask the maids of friends or family whether they knew of anyone who was looking for work. Often, those maids would contact their hometown relatives to find parents willing to allow their children to live and work in the city. In return, the families they worked for would ensure the young maids had free room and board and an opportunity to attend school—usually free public school at night. This type of work arrangement was largely unregulated when I was growing up and although the Peruvian government has made significant efforts to regulate it, this process continues in many parts of the country. So when I say that I grew up with household help, I am not implying that my family had money. I am saying that my family was more privileged than those living in poverty.

Without offering a full, detailed comparative analysis of Peru and the United States, it would be difficult for me to fully explain the differences between the Peruvian and the American middle classes. In truth, they are very different. It would be like comparing apples to bananas, or better yet, rap to merengue. They are the middle classes of very different countries, and the markers for determining who is middle class in each country are very different. For example, a marker to determine whether a person is middle class in the United States is whether that person has a college degree, while in Peru, a large number of middle-class Peruvians do not possess such a degree. In the United States, having a washer and dryer, an HVAC system, or being able to afford a vehicle for each member of the family is typical for a middle-class family. In Peru, in 2000, most middle-class families did not have washer and dryers. Even today, most people in Peru do not have HVAC systems, and many middle-class Peruvians do not own a car. Another interesting difference is that while in the United States, private schools are often reserved for the upper-middle class or the wealthy, attending private high school is more common for Peruvian middle-class students. So, before you get confused when I say that my Peruvian family was middle class, just remember that I am referring to the middle class of a developing South American country during a time when a large number of Peruvians lived below the poverty line.

After I finished breakfast, I left my dirty bowl on the table, assuming that the maid would pick it up later, and walked to the bathroom to get ready. Unfortunately, Heather was taking a shower, and Macy was already waiting at the bathroom door. Her face clearly expressed her annoyance. With two teenage girls sharing a bathroom, things could get a bit tricky in the morning. I would clearly have to wait for a while to get in there, so I went back to my room.

Once Heather and Macy were done getting ready, I slipped into the bathroom. I had brought shampoo, conditioner, and a bar of soap from Peru, though I should have assumed that my host family would have toiletries for me. In fact, the bathtub was filled with all sorts of colorful shampoo bottles, conditioners, body washes, sponges, and other personal cleaning items, many of which I had never seen before. There was also a large assortment of perfumes and makeup. It was a small bathroom, so it was quite crowded. *Do they really need this many shampoos and conditioners? This is just for two people*, I thought, surveying the space.

In Peru, I'd had my own bathroom, and there wasn't much in it: just shampoo, conditioner, a bar of soap, a toothbrush, toothpaste, toilet paper, a big towel, and a hand towel. That was it. At the time, I assumed that having a large number of toiletries was an American thing, although I later learned that the number of toiletries is—like it is with most things—a personal choice.

While I showered, I tried not to move any of the precariously placed bottles in the tub. I failed, and when I was done showering, I picked up all of the bottles I had knocked over.

Grabbing a large towel, I dried off and retreated to my room, where I got dressed in a cotton tee shirt and a pair of jeans. I grabbed my backpack and a thin sweatshirt and headed to the living room to wait for Heather, who was my ride to school.

I hadn't called my family back home in Peru yet. I desperately wanted to speak with them, but I didn't know how. I didn't have a cell phone, and I knew international phone calls were expensive. I needed to ask someone in the house whether I could use the phone, but I was too shy. Besides, even if I weren't shy, I couldn't carry out a fluent conversation in English with anyone. Although Heather had spent some time in Argentina through an exchange program, she didn't like her accent and didn't speak Spanish to me. James had spent a year in Peru and was fluent in Spanish, but he didn't live in the house. Carrie, Edward, and Macy could barely say "*Hola*," "*Gracias*," and "*Por favor*."

As I pondered my situation, Macy entered the living room and turned on the TV. She was in middle school and was waiting for my host mom, who was a nurse, to take her to school on Carrie's way to work. *Saved by the Bell*, one of my favorite shows of the 1990s, was on. The show was in English though, so I didn't understand a word. They spoke too quickly for me, and their voices sounded different from what I was used to. I missed the version dubbed into Spanish that I had grown up watching.

"*Vamos, Santiago*," Heather said as she stormed out of her room in a hurry.

I followed her out of the house, and it was so cold, I could see my breath. I jumped into the front passenger seat of her car, and it felt like I was sitting on a slab of ice. Her car radio played pop music, and I recognized some of the songs because they had been on Peruvian radio as well. I couldn't sing along with them, though. It took us fifteen minutes to get to school. Heather and I finally talked a bit in Spanish. Her Spanish was a little rusty, but I could understand her. I also observed the white landscape all around us. It was mostly farmland covered by snow, with a house here and there and some trees along the road.

This was my first day of school, and I would be the "new guy." The new "foreign" guy. I knew this experience would be different from anything I had done before, and I was anxious. I would be attending a co-ed public school in a small American town. In Peru, I went to an all-male private Jesuit Catholic school in a big city. I was wearing a sweatshirt, tee shirt, and jeans. In Arequipa, I wore a uniform every day.

When we arrived at the high school, I gazed at the hundreds of cars parked outside the building. This was another thing I wasn't used to, as most of my Peruvian friends—like me—couldn't drive and had to take public transportation to school. In Peru, the driving age is eighteen.

We had to park far from the school entrance and walk in the cold for a couple of minutes. Again, I could see my breath. I had never been able to do that before, and although it was fascinating at first, it quickly got old. Being able to see your breath only meant one thing to me: it was too cold to be outside.

Once inside the school, two of Heather's girlfriends approached us, and she introduced me to them. I gave each of them a kiss on the cheek. In return, I got a strange look. One of them even took a step back. They laughed and giggled, but I didn't know why.

In Peru, when a boy is introduced to a girl, he gives her a kiss on the cheek. When meeting other boys, we shake hands. It's simply a Peruvian social norm. Other South American countries have different rules. For example, in Argentina, the kiss is gender-neutral, and everyone gets a kiss on the cheek.

As we walked around the school, I could tell people were staring at me. I thought it was because I was the new guy, but that wasn't it. It didn't take me long to realize that most of the school's population was white, and I stood out like a sore thumb. In addition, I had spent a few days at the beach in Peru before traveling to Iowa, so I had an impressive tan. I definitely looked different from those around me.

Heather and I first headed to the principal's office. She introduced me to some school officials before we met with my counselor. They all smiled and said a few words to me. I smiled back a lot.

"Santiago, let's go pick out your classes," Heather said in broken Spanish as she directed me to the counselor's office.

What? I can pick my own classes? Why would they let a seventeen-year-old pick his own classes? I thought. In Peru, the coursework is the same for every student, and it usually includes math, literature, physics, chemistry, geography, art, religion, a foreign language, and physical education. There is no selecting one's own classes.

Heather took me to my counselor's office, but she was in a hurry to take care of some things, so I walked into the office by myself. I noticed that the counselor's name, Amy, was on a nameplate on her desk. She was on the phone when I walked in, so I sat down and waited for her to finish her call. Once off the phone, Amy introduced herself and handed me a sheet with a list of classes.

As she tried to explain the sheet's contents, I stopped her. "I don't speak English. I'm sorry," I said in broken English.

The look on her face was priceless. She put a hand on her forehead and shook her head. Then she politely took the sheet back and pointed at the list of classes with her pen.

Amy then lifted one hand and used the universal code for displaying numbers: her fingers. "Five," she said, holding up five fingers. Then she handed me the sheet again.

"Okay," I responded with a nervous smile. I assumed that Amy wanted me to pick five classes. *What should I do? Should I be responsible and take some challenging classes? Or should I take fun ones?* I asked myself.

Two required classes appeared to have already been selected for me: algebra and English. Although I had already taken algebra during my senior year of high school in Peru, I could not relay that fact to my counselor. Like many exchange students from South America who join the exchange program, I had already graduated from my Peruvian high school before attending Mount Vernon.

For the elective classes, I chose photography, computer skills (typing), world history, architecture (a planning and design class), and Spanish. I took Spanish because a Peruvian friend had told me that it would help me learn English. It seemed like a contrarian view, but I went along with it.

I handed my sheet back to Amy, and she glanced over it and said, "Okay," with a smile. She then gave me the student handbook and a piece of paper with my locker number and code. With that, she led me out of her office. She tried to give me a tour of the school, but due to the language barrier, I didn't understand much of what she said. Instead, I used the time to become familiar with my surroundings and find my locker. Luckily it wasn't a big high school. It somewhat reminded me of Bayside High School, the school from *Saved by the Bell*.

A few minutes into our tour, the bell rang, and Amy took me back to the principal's office, where Heather was waiting for me. My host sister grabbed my class schedule and walked me to my first class, which was algebra.

The algebra teacher, Mr. Smithson, was a retired college professor. In broken Spanish, Heather told me that his classes were hard and that he had a reputation for being a hothead, which made me nervous. I walked into the classroom and waited for the other students to sit at their desks. I assumed that each student had an assigned desk, as we did in Peru. I later learned that there was no assigned seating. Once everyone was settled, I noticed that there was an empty desk in the back row, so I took it.

Before getting started with class, Mr. Smithson called my name and asked me a question. I shook my head and told him that I didn't speak English. Everyone laughed. He wasn't impressed. He opened a bookcase, took out a book, and handed it to me. Inside the book was a syllabus. I glanced at both and recognized many of the words in the syllabus and the equations in the book. Unlike English or Spanish, math is a universal language.

The class was small. There were no more than fifteen students in the room. Mount Vernon was a small school. In fact, the senior class of 2000 had around seventy students. Two of my classmates were wearing baseball hats, backward. At my school in Peru, wearing hats in class was prohibited. I also noticed that the girl sitting next to me spent most of class exchanging notes with her friend. They didn't pay much attention to Mr. Smithson, though everyone else did.

At the end of class, the bell rang and I walked to my locker. I couldn't open it. I'd never had a locker in Peru and had to carry my books to school in my backpack every day, so this was yet another new experience for me. As I tried to master the art of putting in the locker combination again, I noticed a tall man walking toward me.

"*Hola, Santiago. Mi nombre es Señor Anderson. Soy el profesor de Español,*" he said. He was one of the Spanish teachers, and I noticed that he didn't have a strong accent. I later found out that he had lived in Colombia for a few years.

Mr. Anderson gave me a permission slip to skip my next class, English, and explained that he had spoken with the principal about getting me acquainted with the school, so he took me to his classroom. He read over my class schedule and told me that my Spanish class was with him. He was a Yale University graduate, married to a Colombian woman, and had no kids. He and his wife shared a passion for teaching. He drew a map of the school for me and included the location of my classes, with everything labeled in Spanish. "Let's go. I'll give you a tour," he said in Spanish. Although I'd just had a tour of the school, this time I had a map with my classes on it and someone I could understand. Finally finding someone who spoke the same language as me was comforting.

We walked around the school, and when we arrived at the gymnasium, Mr. Anderson asked if I liked sports. I told him that I had been part of the track and field team in Peru and that I enjoyed playing soccer. He encouraged me to try out for either of those sports, saying, "It would be a good way to meet people."

I didn't tell Mr. Anderson that I had been a national track and field champion back home. I wanted to take a break from running and do something different.

He mentioned that this was the first time the high school would have a soccer team of its own. In the past, it had combined with another school to form a team.

"Maybe I'll try out for soccer," I said.

The bell rang again, and it was time for my Spanish class. We walked back to Mr. Anderson's classroom, and he introduced me to the other students. He gave me a textbook and a worksheet with some exercises. He then explained how past tense verbs are formed in Spanish and gave us time to complete the worksheet. Although I had to use my dictionary to translate many of the English words into Spanish, I completed the worksheet before the bell rang again.

It was now lunchtime. Mr. Anderson walked me to the cafeteria, where I met Heather. She was sitting with two of her girlfriends I had not met yet. As I had done earlier, I gave each girl a kiss on the cheek when Heather introduced us. They didn't kiss me back, and one of them blushed. Heather gave me a look, the kind you get when you do something strange. I shrugged it off and sat down next to them.

When lunch was over, I grabbed my map and headed to my next classes. First up was world history, then architecture, and then photography. The computer skills class was my first class of the day, but I had missed it because I was with the counselor. I received books for all the classes, but it was difficult to follow my teachers. They spoke too quickly for me.

I thought about all the books I had received on that day. All of them for free. In Peru, schools don't provide students with books. Before the school year starts, students receive a list of all required textbooks for the year, and then they and their parents buy them at a bookstore. That morning, I had gone to school with a notebook and a pen, and now I had a backpack full of books.

After the last bell of the day, I walked to my locker to drop off my books and found Heather there, waiting for me to go home. She asked how my day had gone, and I told her that it was good, but that I was tired.

As we headed for the doors, a blonde girl shouted, "Heather, wait," and ran toward us.

"Santiago, this is my cousin Lacy," Heather said in Spanish. I approached Lacy and tried to give her a kiss on the cheek, but she took a step back.

"Wow," she said, laughing a bit.

What is going on? Do I smell or something? I wondered. I placed my hand on my mouth and checked my breath. It seemed fine.

Heather and Lacy talked to each other in English for a few moments, but it was so fast, it sounded like gibberish to me. They then introduced me to three other girls who walked by, all sporting track and field sweatshirts. I tried to give each a friendly kiss and received a mixed response. One kissed me back, but the other two took a step back. *Did I forget to put deodorant on this morning?* I moved my head to the right, trying to smell my armpit without them noticing. I did the same with the left side. I smelled fine.

At this point, I was embarrassed and just wanted to leave. After a few awkward minutes, we walked out to the parking lot. Lacy rode with us, so I climbed into the car's back seat.

What happened today? Why did all these girls react that way? All I knew was that I wasn't going to kiss any more girls. Either they didn't like foreign guys, or people just didn't do that here.

After Heather dropped Lacy off at her house, she confirmed my suspicions. "Santiago, for tomorrow, just remember one thing: no more kissing. Girls don't do that here. Shake hands instead, you dork," she said in Spanish, with a warm smile that softened the embarrassing directive.

Brilliant. That information would have come in handy much sooner. I was embarrassed, but we were able to laugh about it together. Even though I had watched American movies and television in the past, I had never paid much attention to how people said hi to each other. A friendly kiss on the cheek had been my automatic response when meeting women. It took me that embarrassing day to realize that what I was doing was not customary in my new world.

When we got home, I walked into my room, and it was a mess. My bed hadn't been made, my clothes were where I had left them in the morning, and the glass of water I had left on my nightstand was still sitting there, half full. *Where in the world is the maid?* I wondered.

Chapter Five
DIRTY DISHES AND DIRTY LAUNDRY

January 22, 2000

It was a cold and gloomy Saturday morning. My first week in Iowa had passed, and I hadn't seen the Novaks' maid yet. I was beginning to suspect that either my host family didn't have outside help or the help only came on weekends.

In Arequipa, I never had to wash the dishes. We had a maid for that. I didn't have to wash my own clothes. A lady came to our house every weekend to do that. I never had to clean my room. Again, someone else did that.

So, like magic, my bedroom back home in Peru was always clean and organized. However, in Iowa, my room was a disaster. My bed was permanently unmade, and by the end of my first week there, I had accumulated a small mountain of dirty clothes, and I didn't know what to do with them. Plus, I had been living out of my suitcase because I hadn't put everything away yet—I still hadn't worked up the courage to ask my host family to put the rifles and ammo someplace else so I could make use of the dresser and the wardrobe. Frankly, my room was beginning to smell.

That Saturday morning, I walked into the kitchen and noticed that no one else was up yet. I grabbed a bowl and poured some cereal and milk into it. While I loved the convenience of a quick meal, I was starting to wonder if I would be having the same breakfast each day for the whole year.

I took my Spanish-English dictionary with me to the kitchen table. I needed to ask Carrie what time the maid arrived on weekends, so I prepared a script and practiced it for a few minutes. Since Heather had spent the night at Lacy's home, she wouldn't be there to help me translate.

After a while, I heard someone walk into the kitchen. It was Carrie. "Good morning!" I shouted. I've always been a morning person, but I might have been a bit too chipper for a Saturday morning.

"Hi, Santiago," she responded with a forced smile. Carrie wasn't a morning person, and it showed. She appeared to still be half asleep.

"Where is the maid?" I asked.

Carrie stopped in her tracks. She didn't seem to understand my question. "What?" she asked.

I repeated the question, trying to say it with a better accent, so I didn't roll my r's as much.

She laughed, and I could tell she was laughing in disbelief. "No maid, Santiago. No maid," she said. She pointed at my dirty bowl, the one she had been picking up for the past week, and took it to the sink. "You, Santiago." She rinsed it and put it in the dishwasher. Then she grabbed the cereal box I had left on the kitchen table. "You," she said, putting it away. She then turned and walked me to my room, opened the door, and shook her head. Although she was smiling, I could tell she was frustrated.

She said a few more words, but I could not understand all of them. By now I realized that the Novaks didn't have a maid, but I could not understand what else she wanted from me. I handed her a piece of paper and told her to write what she wanted to say. It would be easier for me to translate that way.

"Santiago, you have to clean up after yourself. Please start by cleaning your room," she wrote. The smiley face she added after that message didn't alleviate my embarrassment. She had been cleaning up after me for the past week, and I hadn't thanked her once.

"I am sorry," I wrote on the same piece of paper.

Carrie read it, smiled, and grabbed the pen. "It's okay," she wrote, adding another smiley face.

This meant that I would have to make my bed, pick up my clothes, clean my room, and make my own breakfast each day. After seventeen years of not having to clean up after myself, I would have to learn a new habit. Plus, since there was no maid, that probably meant there was no laundry lady, either. I had never done laundry before, so this would be a challenge. I assumed this would be especially tricky because it was so cold outside.

In Peru, a lady came to our house every week to wash our clothes. She would arrive around seven in the morning every Saturday to wash—by hand—a giant load of laundry, and it took most of the day. After she was done washing our clothes, she would hang them on a couple of ropes strategically placed on the roof, where they would line-dry. The whole process was done outside. In Mount Vernon, I was worried that I would have to wash my clothes by hand and then hang them up to dry outside in the freezing Iowa cold. Luckily, I soon realized that my American family neither washed nor dried their clothes outside.

Carrie brought a basket to my room and helped me put my dirty clothes in it. Then she took me to the basement of the house and pointed at two machines: a washer and a dryer. I had never used such devices before because, at the time, washers and dryers were reserved for the wealthy in Peru. Most middle-class families didn't have them.

Because writing notes on a piece of paper and translating them back and forth wasn't an efficient method of communication, Carrie showed me how to use these machines by example. She grabbed a basket full of Edward's clothes and used them to demonstrate the process.

After Carrie placed Edward's clothes in the washer and started the machine, Edward called her to come help him with something upstairs. She went up to see what he needed, but I stayed in the basement, which was full of random objects. Most Peruvian homes don't have a basement, so this space was a mystery to me. I decided to explore.

In one corner, I found three deer heads accumulating dust and several containers piled on top of each other. One was full of Christmas decorations, and another contained a bunch of plastic pumpkins. Two other containers had what appeared to be summer clothing, which gave me some hope that the weather would eventually get warmer. One small container, which was full of old books, caught my attention. I perused the books with delight and noticed some familiar names: Ernest Hemingway, Mark Twain, and F. Scott Fitzgerald, among others. I took that small container to my room. I hoped no one cared.

A short while later, Carrie called my name. She was heading back down to the basement and was ready to continue my laundry lesson. Edward's clothes were now washed, and Carrie wanted to show me how to use the dryer. I was perplexed by how quickly the washer had washed all those clothes. That load would have taken hours for my Peruvian laundry lady. Carrie pointed at the dryer, opened the door, and put Edward's wet clothes in it. Then she closed the door and turned it on. That was it.

That's so easy, I thought.

With that done, we went upstairs, and Carrie and Edward grabbed a couple of winter coats. They had to drive to Cedar Rapids to run some errands. I opted to stay home with Macy, who was still asleep.

After they left, I returned to the basement to wash my own clothes. I put all my clothes in the washer, added the detergent, pressed the correct buttons on the machine, and turned it on. It took about forty-five minutes for me to realize that I had made a fatal mistake. When Carrie explained how to use the washer, I had focused more on the technical aspects of the machine itself. I didn't focus on the necessary step of separating whites from darks. I had mixed my white cotton tee shirts with some new red and green shirts. When I opened the washer, I realized that I had become the owner of an assortment of "tie-dyed" shirts. Fortunately, not all of the clothes were affected by this rookie mistake, but the unaffected clothes would soon meet their demise with the application of hot air.

The dryer came with its own set of challenges. In Arequipa, most people line-dry their clothes, so most clothing doesn't shrink. It's not something I even considered.

I followed Carrie's instructions and put my wet clothes in the dryer, then pressed the 'Start' button and walked away. Sixty minutes later, I came back to a load of soft, warm clothing. I put my things in the basket and took them up to my room to fold. I started with a tee shirt, but it seemed smaller than I remembered. *Oh no*, I thought, *did I accidentally mix my host sister's clothes in with mine?* I couldn't believe I would be that absent-minded, but it seemed to be the only logical answer.

I examined all the shirts, and they were indeed all mine, but when I tried one of them on, it was tight on me. I looked in the mirror and saw that it fit like a muscle shirt—but without the muscles. My one-hundred-percent cotton shirts were no match for an American dryer set on high. Several of them had shrunk.

During the next few hours, I organized and cleaned my room. I decided to take the initiative and move some of the rifles to the garage to make space for some of my clothes that hadn't shrunk. My room became habitable again.

A few hours later, I heard Carrie and Edward pulling in the driveway and wrote another note for Carrie. As soon as she walked into the house, I showed Carrie my shrunken tie-dye shirts and handed her my note: "Can you take me shopping?"

Chapter Six
FREEZING FOOD IN THE FROZEN TUNDRA

January 27, 2000

Doing laundry and cleaning up after myself were not difficult tasks, even though I ended up having to buy some new clothes as part of the learning process. Eating well, however, was different. I knew very little about nutrition, as I had never had to prepare or even select my own food before. Back in Peru, these tasks had always been done for me as well.

In Arequipa, I woke up every day to a freshly made breakfast. Jacinta, our maid, would get up before sunrise to buy bread from the local *bodega*. She would put the warm bread in a small wooden basket in the middle of the table and cover it with a thin piece of cloth. To go with this fresh bread, we usually had a good spread of items, including ham, cheese, butter, avocado, and black olives. Depending on the season, Jacinta would either prepare banana or strawberry smoothies or squeeze a few oranges into orange juice. Most days, I also had a cup of warm milk with some sugar and coffee mixed in.

For the most part, Peruvians have a heavy lunch with two courses: a bowl of soup and an entree. Every morning, Jacinta would talk to my mother about what she would like to have for lunch. If we were missing an ingredient, Jacinta would go to the market or to the closest *bodega* to buy it. Both were located just a few blocks from our home. At the time, most Peruvian companies allowed their employees to take a break of two or three hours in the middle of the workday, so my parents would come home to eat lunch and take a *siesta*.

Fresh ingredients are key for Peruvian cooking. Peruvian *ceviche*, the most iconic Peruvian dish—and not to be confused with other Latin American *ceviches*—is prepared with fresh raw fish, sliced red onions, hot peppers, cilantro, and salt and marinated with freshly squeezed key lime juice. It's important that all these ingredients be fresh. To achieve an acceptable level of freshness, most Peruvian families visit the market or the local *bodega* at least once a week. Many go daily. Although globalization is beginning to meddle with that tradition, freezing food is not common. Fresh ingredients and daily home cooking are still the primary choices for making Peruvian food.

Also, unlike their American counterparts, Peruvian schools don't generally serve lunch, so students have to bring some sort of lunch bag to school. Wealthier parents give their kids money to purchase snacks at the school kiosk in an attempt to keep them fed until lunch. In my case, school ran from eight a.m. to two p.m., so I didn't get to have lunch until around three p.m. when I got home. This meant that after the school day was over, one often saw lots of "hungry" Peruvian kids running around the school hallways, eager to go home and eat.

In addition, in Peru, the evening meal is generally on the lighter side. Most families eat leftovers from lunch, have tea and a piece of bread, or prepare small sandwiches. Unlike with many Iowa families, dinner (or supper, as my host family called it) isn't the main meal of the day in Peru.

I've always considered Peruvian cuisine to be a delicious treat that everyone must experience at least once. Peru's biodiversity and rich cultural history make its food a unique experience. Peruvians harvest products from the coast, the Andean mountains, and the jungle and combine these ingredients with diverse culinary traditions. Italian and Asian cuisines hold strong influence in Peru, as well as local traditions, and the spices found there make for a unique assortment of flavors. It includes dishes such as *ceviche*, *lomo saltado*, *ají de gallina*, *chupe de camarones*, *rocoto relleno*, *causa*, *adobo*, *anticuchos*, *arroz chaufa*, *chilcano*, *locro*, *ocopa*, and *papa a la huancaína*, among many others.

During my first two weeks in Iowa, I mostly ate cereal for breakfast. This wasn't necessarily a bad thing, as my host family had a large assortment of cereal boxes in their pantry. A few times, my host parents cooked scrambled eggs and bacon, which they served with toasted bread. Although it was different for me, I welcomed it. I especially enjoyed the bacon, which wasn't a traditional part of my Peruvian breakfast. Although it felt greasy, it was delicious.

For lunch, I ate at school during the week. Although it took me a couple of days to figure it out, I learned the process: walk to the cafeteria, grab a tray, and stand in line to get food. The school cafeteria had a different menu every day. I either sat with Heather or with other exchange students, most of whom were from Europe and Asia. Since I couldn't say much, I observed. I noticed that there was a table full of athletes. There was also one filled with those who did not appear to be athletically inclined—kids who looked like the stereotypical geeks from the nineties. Another table was made up of students who wore long black shirts and pants, which I found intriguing. There was also a table filled with students who appeared to think of school as a fashion show, with girls wearing more makeup than Britney Spears in her newest MTV video.

The food, although filling, didn't have much flavor. My favorite day was when the school cafeteria had its "Italian" menu, which included pizza, a couple pieces of garlic bread, some dipping sauce, and salad.

For dinner, my host mother generally prepared meals for the family, often with frozen ingredients.

The concept of freezing meals and ingredients was new to me, but my host family relied on it a great deal. There were two big freezers in our garage. One stored what I thought was an entire cow cut into pieces, though I later learned it wasn't a whole cow—just half of one. Like many Iowa farmers, my host parents either had one of their cows butchered or bought meat from another farmer and froze it each fall. Many would buy a "quarter," some would purchase a "half," and some, I assume, bought a "whole" cow.

This business of freezing meat was efficient, cost-effective, and convenient. In Iowa, most people have to drive to the grocery store, so buying in bulk and freezing seems like the perfect alternative to making daily trips to the store. Plus, not only is it cheaper to buy meat in bulk, but buyers can choose the farmer from whom they buy their meat. It helps the local economy, and many times, buyers and sellers build long-lasting relationships.

Meat wasn't the only food that my host family stored in their freezers. The other freezer contained bread, fruit, vegetables, and an assortment of frozen meals. Again, this was all new to me, but it made sense. With those bitterly cold and snowy Iowa winters, who would want to make an extra trip to town to get food?

Freezing food was one thing, but consuming frozen meals was another. Although convenient, frozen meals had a major downside for me: most lacked flavor. Luckily, it seemed that eating frozen meals was the exception, rather than the norm, for my host family.

I enjoyed my host parents' cooking, especially when they made a bean-based Mexican dish called chili. I couldn't stop sweating the first time I tried it, as the Novaks liked their chili spicy. My host parents always made so much food that we had plenty of leftovers. They put the leftovers in containers, some of which ended up in the fridge, but most of which ended up in—you probably already guessed it—the freezer.

Chapter Seven
THE WIND HURTS MY FACE

February 9, 2000

Iowa, in February, is cold. Every time I walked out the door, the cold air immediately penetrated my clothes, and when I took a breath, the cold air cut my lungs like a knife. For those used to living in the Northern Hemisphere, this may sound like an exaggeration, but as someone who grew up in a warmer climate, it's an accurate description of my first experience with the outdoor freezer Iowans call home.

"Santiago, you'll get used to it," Heather kept assuring me in Spanish.

I had serious doubts about that. *No one can get used to this type of weather*, I thought.

To make matters even more interesting, a few weeks before I arrived in the United States, I learned that I was allergic to cold temperatures. While swimming in the cold ocean waters of Camaná, a Peruvian coastal town on the Pacific Ocean, I developed a skin condition called "cold urticaria," in which reddish spots appeared on my skin. My parents took me to the doctor, who explained that I was indeed allergic to the cold. If left untreated, it could lead to low blood pressure and even fainting.

"Don't worry, Santiago," my doctor had assured me at the time. "Unless you spend the winter in towns with higher altitudes than Arequipa, you'll have no issues." In Peru, higher altitudes usually meant lower temperatures. Unfortunately, when he gave me his "Don't worry," diagnosis, my doctor didn't know I was moving to Iowa—a place at a lower altitude than Arequipa, but with brutally cold winters.

Due to my allergy, I had to "winterize" myself before venturing outdoors while temperatures remained below forty degrees. This meant I had to wear layer upon layer of clothing so my internal heat wouldn't leave my body and cause rashes.

On the average winter day, just to leave the house, I had to wear long, thick socks, boots, a pair of *vicuña* wool underpants, jeans or sweatpants, an undershirt, a tee shirt, a sweatshirt, a heavy coat, a scarf, and earmuffs or ear warmers. Some clothing I brought from Peru and some I borrowed from my host family, but some I had to buy in Iowa. It took me longer to dress than to walk from the house to Heather's car in the driveway. It had to be done though, as I didn't want to develop an allergic reaction because of inadequate "winterization."

Inside my Iowa home, however, I could generally wear shorts and tee shirts without any problems. This was due to the warm air that flowed out of special grated holes in the walls and ceiling. They call it a heating, ventilation, and air-conditioning system, or "HVAC." I had never experienced one before moving to Iowa.

In Peru, most homes don't have HVAC systems. When it's cold outside, it's cold inside, so every winter, thousands of people living in the Andes suffer from prolonged exposure to cold temperatures. This primarily affects children and the elderly, and while an average winter causes plenty of hardships for those living in high altitudes, an unusually cold one can be deadly. In the summer, since most homes don't have AC systems, hot temperatures follow you everywhere. Fortunately, in Iowa, almost all homes are blessed with HVAC systems, and most Americans seem to take this technology for granted. In the winter, even if the HVAC doesn't work, most households can burn wood in their fireplaces.

For me, this meant that as long as I stayed inside my Iowa home, I wouldn't develop a rash. While venturing outdoors, however, if I weren't appropriately dressed, my skin would begin to itch. So, when my host brother James took me ice fishing, I learned what Iowa's cold temperatures could truly do to my sensitive skin.

Ice fishing is simple: you cut an opening in the ice on a frozen lake or pond, lower fishing lines and hooks into the opening, and wait. My host family had a small pond on their farm, and every summer, they would add fish to it so they could fish in the winter.

The only type of fishing I had ever done in Peru was in the Pacific Ocean. During the summer months, while vacationing at the beach, my friends and I would get together at sunrise and walk to a spot with large rocks by the water, where we knew fish would congregate. Then we would tie a hook to a line and throw it as far into the ocean as we could with our bare hands. After a successful throw, we would tie the other end of the line to a heavy rock and wait. Although we generally ended up empty-handed, sometimes we got lucky, and a fish would bite.

When James and I walked to the icy pond that morning to go ice fishing, the picture was very different. It was a cloudy, dry, and cold day. We brought along a couple of chairs and a machine to cut the opening in the ice. James also brought a backpack with fishing equipment, a couple of insulated thermoses with hot coffee, and two buckets: one full of worms and an empty one for the fish we would catch.

Initially, the whole process was exciting because it was so different. James cut a hole in the ice, and we placed our chairs around it. We prepared our fishing rods and put worms on the hooks. Then we lowered the hooks into the water and waited. This is when things started to go south for me. It's one thing to sit around and wait for fish to bite during the spring or summer, when outdoor temperatures are generally above sixty degrees Fahrenheit. It's another thing to wait outside when temperatures are in the teens and you can see your breath.

James had planned on spending three or four hours on the ice, but after thirty minutes outside, I started to feel terrible. I had "winterized" myself as usual, but it didn't matter. The cold air penetrated all my layers of clothing, and it felt like a cold knife was cutting through my bones. My face not only started to itch; it also hurt. Soon, the wind picked up, and I felt as if someone were throwing small darts at my face.

"Are you okay, Santiago? Your face is turning bright red," James said in Spanish with a concerned look. I had not told my host family about my cold allergy, so James didn't know why I was experiencing that reaction.

"I'm not. How much longer are we going to be here?" I asked, clearly miserable.

"Let's go home now. You're starting to worry me," he said.

We packed up and walked back to the house. At that point, my entire body was itching painfully, and my face hurt even more. I could only think about splashing warm water onto it, wrapping myself in a blanket, and drinking hot tea.

How can I possibly live in a place where the wind hurts my face? I thought as we walked into the house.

Chapter Eight
COPING

March 1, 2000

In Peru, like most city dwellers, I relied on a mixture of private and public transportation. When my parents couldn't take me somewhere, I would either take a bus or a taxi. My parents paid a lady to take me to and from the high school every day. If I had to stay at school for soccer or track practice, I would take a city bus home. Meeting up with friends and family wasn't an issue: if they lived far from me, I could take a cab to go hang out, and if they lived nearby, I could just walk down the street to see them.

Iowa was different. Unless you lived in town, you needed a car—and even those who lived in town generally had cars. Most of the students at Mount Vernon High School had their own vehicles. Heather and Carrie had sedans. Edward and James drove trucks.

In Peru, you have to be eighteen years old to apply for a license, but in Iowa, students can get a driving permit at fourteen. Most have a license at sixteen. It wasn't hard to understand why, though. In rural communities, there isn't adequate public transportation. People have to travel a few miles to go to school, get groceries, and meet other people.

Unless you lived in-town, walking places is pretty much impossible.

Having a car in Iowa isn't only necessary; it also provides one with a certain degree of freedom. It gives you the independence to go places. Unfortunately, as an exchange student, I wasn't allowed to operate a motor vehicle. This made sense: the exchange program didn't want a bunch of exchange students getting in car accidents. Unfortunately, this meant that, in the United States, I was dependent on others for rides. Thus far, I had mostly relied on Heather, Carrie, and Edward for trips, but I knew I needed to expand my social network of potential rides. Both Carrie and Edward worked, and Heather usually had a busy schedule. Besides, they were not my chauffeurs. This left me with the problem of wondering how I could increase the number of people who could take me places. I could make friends and rely on them for rides, but how could I make friends when I could barely speak the language? Even though I was surrounded by people all the time, I felt isolated due to the language barrier. I had to find a way to learn the language faster. But how?

When I was at home, Edward was usually around in the mornings. He worked the night shift at a factory in Cedar Rapids and slept in the afternoon. He enjoyed watching television with me in the living room, and he showed me how to turn on the closed-captioning option that was available for most shows. After that, I realized that watching TV was an excellent way to learn English. I regularly watched *Friends*, *Saved by the Bell*, *Seinfeld*, and even *The Golden Girls*. I particularly enjoyed American comedies, which is probably why I developed a wry sense of humor.

In school, people slowly started to notice me, and some began to say hello in the halls. Every morning, the guy who used the locker next to mine greeted me with, "Hi, Santiago. How are you?"

I usually responded with a simple, "Good. How are you?" I didn't even know his name. I would have loved to ask, but I didn't dare start a conversation yet. I would practice my English at home, in my room, for hours, but I still couldn't muster the courage to speak at school.

*   *   *

It had been a couple of months since my arrival, and I still couldn't speak much English. I was beginning to understand it, but I didn't feel confident enough to speak it in return. I started to wonder if I would ever feel confident enough to do so. I was sure I would. I just wished I could master it faster.

Calling home was also a challenge. Although I was able to call my mother a few days after I arrived in Iowa, I didn't call Peru often because my host family didn't have a long-distance calling plan. The local grocery store sold international phone cards, and although they were expensive, I bought a couple. A five-dollar phone card would enable me to make a five-minute call to Peru, so I usually just called my mother. I had tried calling my father, but he hadn't responded to my phone calls yet. My parents were separated, so if I wanted to speak to both of them, I had to make two calls. I realized that calling home could get expensive quickly, so I only spoke with my family on special occasions. Otherwise, I would have gone broke trying to call home.

Unlike most of the European and Asian exchange students I knew, I didn't have a credit card, and I did not receive any money from my Peruvian family during my year in the United States. Although my parents had enjoyed several years of relative financial abundance, after their separation, they lost the family business, and our finances began to worsen. Luckily, as part of the exchange program, I received one hundred dollars each month as an allowance. Since I had brought about two hundred dollars with me from Peru—which represented my entire life savings at the time—this seemed like a lot of money. Still, this money was intended for my personal expenses, and I couldn't spend it all on phone cards.

I tried to chat with my family online as much as I could, but it wasn't the same as hearing their voices. I used MSN Messenger, but the Novaks' dial-up Internet connection was slow, and I lost connectivity often.

I soon realized that the hardest part of moving to another country without knowing the language, without being able to interact with most people, and without having constant communication with my Peruvian family back home was the loneliness I experienced. I had never been a "loner" back home and had always been surrounded by my family and good friends with whom I could communicate freely. Even though I was rarely alone in Mount Vernon, I couldn't communicate well. I had so much to say, but I struggled to connect with other people. The language barrier was a major issue, and I frequently felt incredibly lonely. Often, I simply wanted to pack my bags and go back to Peru.

For the most part, this intense loneliness overtook me at night. On many occasions, I grabbed my pillow and cried myself to sleep. Except for the two deer heads in my room, no one could hear me.

However, going back to Arequipa wasn't an option. Even telling my mother that I felt lonely wouldn't help. I knew that sharing these feelings with her would just hurt her and make her worry. Something needed to change.

As I considered my situation, I grabbed a piece of paper and came up with three options:

- Option One: I could accept defeat and take the next flight back to Lima.

- Option Two: I could continue to feel lonely and regret my decision to come to Iowa for the entire year.

- Option Three: I could try to adapt, learn to live with this loneliness, get over it, and just hope that things would get better.

The first option was unacceptable. I couldn't and wouldn't do that.

Option two was tempting. It would be easy to feel like a helpless victim. I could stay in my room and cry myself to sleep every night. I could get online and chat with my Peruvian friends and family for some comfort. I could tell them that I was lonely and that I needed to chat with them. They would understand and would want to talk. They would support me.

However, by choosing option two, I would be falling into a trap: the trap of living in the United States without being present, of my body being in Iowa, but my mind still in Peru. It would be increasingly difficult to escape my Peruvian life and enjoy my experience in Iowa, creating an endless cycle of loneliness and isolation. I didn't want to do that.

Option three would be the hardest. Choosing it meant that I would need to separate myself from my family, at least for a while. It meant that I couldn't sit in front of the computer all day long, reading Peruvian news or chatting with friends. It meant that I needed to start living—both in mind and in body—in Iowa. How could I do that? I couldn't even talk to the people around me. I couldn't read or watch television like I did back home. I could only observe.

After pondering all this for a while, I chose the third option. I would have to learn how to live with this loneliness, at least for a while. Eventually, I would get over it. I needed to find a way to keep moving forward and to cope.

I made a new list. This one was a to-do list to help me keep my mind off of Peru for a while and to start living in the United States. This list had four bullet points:

- *Learn English*. I had to spend more time studying the language. I needed to start communicating with other people. I had to be courageous.

- *Get out of my comfort zone*. I needed to talk to people using what I learned every day. I had to get out of my shell, quickly. It didn't matter if people didn't understand me at first. I just had to hope that they eventually would.

- *Limit Internet access*. I needed to limit my time online. No more staying up late chatting with my friends in Peru. No more reading about the soccer games back home. I had to restrain myself from checking my email every hour that I was home.

- *Pray*. Praying felt right to me. It was also a way to meditate, to keep my mind in the present, and to be thankful for this opportunity. It was a way for me to stop complaining about my "bad luck." It may not work for everyone, but praying worked for me.

I started doing these four things. I knew it was going to be difficult, but I needed to give myself a chance—a chance to experience the things I had always wanted to, a chance to grow, and a chance to mature.

I had to learn to cope.

Chapter Nine
THE RIPPLE EFFECT

March 7, 2000

After a few weeks of surviving Iowa's cold winter weather, I was relieved when a heat wave came through. When I opened my eyes one morning, I could hear some birds chirping, and when I looked out the window, I saw that the snow had started to melt.

Although it was a Sunday, we didn't have to go to church that morning because the family had gone to mass the previous night. Both the Novaks and I were Catholic, and they took me to the town's Catholic Church with them every weekend. This week, we had attended Saturday night mass, thus fulfilling our obligation for the week.

By the time I finally got up, my host parents and Heather were already gone. The night before, they had invited me to join them at a fundraising breakfast for veterans in Cedar Rapids, but I didn't feel like waking up at seven a.m. to go.

After I got dressed, I walked out into the living room and found Macy watching TV by herself. She was waiting for Tamara, one of her school friends. Tamara was fourteen and had a learner's permit unlike Macy, so she was usually Macy's "designated driver." They were planning to go to the Cedar Rapids mall to buy Christina Aguilera's new CD. I had a feeling they were planning to meet some boys there as well, but I had no proof. Either way, I didn't really care what my youngest host sister was up to in her spare time.

"Santiago, want to go to the mall with us?" Macy asked. I was surprised by the offer, which was nice, especially since I knew she probably didn't want me to go with them.

What would a seventeen-year-old boy do with a fourteen-year-old and a thirteen-year-old girl at the mall? I thought. I told her that I preferred to stay at home.

After eating breakfast, I went back to my room and read for a bit. I had picked up a copy of Anne Frank's *The Diary of a Young Girl* at the school's library, which Mr. Anderson, my Spanish teacher, had recommended. He said that as I began to get a better grasp of the language, it would be good for me to start reading something in English, even if I couldn't fully understand it.

After about thirty minutes of trying to read my book, I heard Tamara walk into the house. She and Macy talked for a few minutes as they got ready to leave. Then Macy shouted, "Bye, Santiago," from the kitchen. She slammed the front door on her way out.

I was now alone in the house. I was struggling with my book, so I set it aside. I had nothing to do and nowhere to go. It had been a while since I got to enjoy a day at home with no one around. Instead of staying inside, I decided to explore the farm. Up to that day, it had been too cold, and I hadn't been able to comfortably explore my new outdoor world.

For many people living in the Midwest, farms are a familiar part of their landscape and livelihood, but I was not used to them. I was a city boy, and most of my friends and family were city people. I grew up surrounded by concrete structures and playing soccer on asphalt. I had been to the zoo before and to the countryside on vacation, and some of my relatives raised chickens and guinea pigs, but I had never lived on a farm.

When I stepped outside, I noticed that the road and driveway were muddy due to the melting snow. That didn't bother me. It was a quiet Sunday morning, and the air was crisp and clean, so I was going to explore no matter what.

As I walked toward the barn, I thought about the times when my father had taken my entire extended family to the Peruvian countryside. We would all ride in three or four cars to a public campground outside the city to spend some time surrounded by nature. Us children would bring our soccer balls and play on whatever field we could find. We would grab two big rocks and use them as goal posts. The grown-ups were in charge of cooking the food while we played. My father would bring our small metal grill and cook for all of us. I enjoyed being outdoors in nature and being able to leave the city for a day, but I never imagined that I would end up living in a farmhouse.

Once I reached the barn, I opened one of the gates and walked around a couple of cows eating hay in a pen beside the barn. My host family did not grow grain, as their land wasn't ideal for corn or soybeans, the two main grain crops in Iowa. They used to raise animals to sell as meat but had quit the business a few years back when corporate farms took over the cattle industry in the state. Their farm was more of what's known as a "hobby farm." This is a smaller farm that does not serve as the family's primary source of food or income. Despite this, Edward still spent a lot of time taking care of it.

The Novaks' farm was unique. They had cows, horses, emus, peacocks, and a burro. They also had a small pond—the scene of my ice-fishing experience—which they stocked with fish, so they could go fishing any time of the year. Wild animals like deer, squirrels, and rabbits also made an occasional appearance.

As I wandered around inside the barn, I thought about my life in Mount Vernon. I had moved to a developed country thinking that I would live in a big city with "city things." Instead, I was living in a farmhouse, outside a small town, and in a state that most Americans considered "flyover country." What had happened? What went wrong? Was this a waste of my time?

Unlike many farms in Iowa, the Novaks' farm was not on flat land. It had some hills, which is why it was not ideal for growing grain crops. It was a bit slippery out, so I grabbed a wooden stick to help me balance on the incline and headed down to the pond, which was at the bottom of a small hill, surrounded by trees. Once I made it close to the water, I sat on a rock and observed my surroundings.

What's the point of being here? I wondered as I stared into the water.

I picked up a stone and threw it into the pond. It skipped across the water a couple of times before it sank. The water was so clean and calm, I could see ripples form on its surface. I waited until the ripples had disappeared and the water was calm again, and then I picked up a bigger stone and threw it in. Once again, ripples formed, and I watched them scatter across the entire pond. This time, as the rock hit the bottom, it stirred up some dirt, and the clear water became muddy. It took a few minutes for the dirt to settle and for the water to become clear again. I threw more stones in the water and watched more ripples form.

It was at that moment that I realized what was happening in my life and why moving to Iowa wasn't merely a coincidence.

Moving to Iowa was like throwing a stone into that pond. I had no idea what I was doing there, but I jumped into it with both feet. My environment—like the environment of the stones I threw—changed in an instant, and I became part of this new place—this new pond. Visiting a new place—or, in my case, moving to a foreign country—is like jumping into that pond. I didn't know whether the water was cold or warm, or whether I would be welcomed or rejected. I was sure of one thing, though: I was that stone making ripples in the water. This was my opportunity to impact the lives of the people around me and to change my own.

Considering this, I asked myself two questions: what kind of ripples am I capable of making? And how much will my life impact those around me?

A few minutes later, I walked back to the house, smiling and thinking about my realization. I was ready to discover how big of a ripple my life could make in this "Iowa pond."

Chapter Ten
JOINING THE TEAM

March 27, 2000

It was now late March, and I could feel the temperature changing. The transition from winter to spring in Iowa was a quick, but treacherous one. Although the temperature went in an upward direction on average, some days I experienced inexplicable drops in temperature. As it got warmer though, the snow melted in a matter of days, the grass magically began to grow again, and green leaves were beginning to fill branches that, for months, had merely been wooden sticks. Everything seemed to be coming back to life.

At school, the track was no longer covered by snow, and after school, I noticed some athletes running laps on it. On other fields, I saw students throwing baseballs back and forth to each other.

Closer to the school building, I noticed some students playing with small colorful bags they called "hacky sacks." Hacky sacks are handmade crocheted balls usually filled with plastic beads. The game they played with these hacky sacks required a few players to stand in a circle, awkwardly kick the sack to each other, and keep it from touching the ground. I had never seen anything like it, so this lively game caught my attention, and I approached the group.

"Santiago, *quieres jugar*?" a student with shaggy blonde hair said, asking me if I wanted to play. It was Noah Sommer, a boy from my Spanish class. His mother, Mrs. Sommer, was an outgoing and upbeat Spanish teacher at the high school. Noah was the most animated of the group and also the best player.

Did I want to play? Of course! "*Sí*," I enthusiastically responded.

During the past few weeks, I had spent most of my time with my host sister Heather and her friends. Heather and I got along well, but we had different interests. This was an excellent opportunity to branch out from my usual crew. Making friends as an exchange student can be difficult, and this is especially true if the exchange student doesn't speak the local language, like me.

Noah introduced me to the other two students he was playing with, David and Snyder. David had been born in Africa but had lived in Mount Vernon for most of his life. His last name was a mouthful: Alamieyeseigha. I decided that I would just call him David and that his last name would have to wait. Snyder was a skinny blonde white boy. He had been born in Minnesota, but his family moved to Iowa when his father got a job at a paper plant in Cedar Rapids.

Noah passed me the hacky sack, and I tried to "juggle" it with my feet. It was harder than it looked. After a few minutes though, I was juggling like an experienced player. Noah was apparently impressed, because he opened his backpack and grabbed a soccer ball. "Can you do that with this?" he asked.

I picked up the soccer ball with my left foot and juggled it for a few minutes. I felt much more confident kicking the soccer ball around than the hacky sack. I passed it to Noah, who kicked it to Snyder, who in turn gave it to David. We didn't say much. We just kicked the ball around for a while. After a few minutes of play, Snyder grabbed his backpack and said a few words to me. However, he said them too quickly, so I didn't understand.

"Sorry, slow down, please," I said. I was beginning to understand English, but people still had to speak slowly for me to understand them. Snyder smiled and spoke to Noah, and they exchanged an unusual handshake. Snyder then also shook my hand and walked away.

"You should join the soccer team. Practice starts tomorrow, after school," Noah said casually. "Snyder thinks you're good."

"Okay," I responded. I tried to remain calm, but it was difficult to hide my excitement.

However, practice after school meant that I needed to get a ride home after practice. I couldn't count on Heather, as she didn't usually stick around after school. My only hope was Carrie. She worked in town until five p.m. every day, so perhaps she could pick me up on her way home from work.

That night at home, I grabbed my dictionary, searched for some words, and wrote a couple of questions on a piece of paper. I handed the note to Carrie: "Soccer practice is tomorrow after school. Can you give me a ride?"

Carrie looked at me and said slowly and carefully, "A ride to the soccer field?" She was aware of my struggle, and she not only spoke to me slowly, but she also used simple words.

"No, no. Here. Home," I responded.

"Yes, Santiago. Sure," she said. I couldn't contain my excitement, and I gave her a hug.

With that, I ran to my room, opened one of my suitcases, and looked for my soccer cleats. They were in a plastic bag, along with my track and field spikes. I had brought both pairs of shoes because I loved both sports, but I was tired of running. I wanted to try something different. This year was about new experiences and trying new things. I had never given soccer a real chance in Peru, so I would do so now in the United States.

*　　*　　*

The next day, I met Noah after school, and he walked me to the locker room, where Snyder and David were already changing. They were all excited because, as Mr. Anderson had told me on my first day, this was the first time Mount Vernon had its own soccer team. The school was small, so in the past, it had to join the nearby Solon High School to have enough players. This year, however, Mount Vernon had enough players to have both varsity and junior varsity teams for boys and girls.

The four of us walked out to the field, and Noah introduced me to a few other players. As we warmed up, I looked around and observed the others there. Some students, like Snyder, were talented, while some struggled to kick the ball straight. It quickly became apparent that there were those who could play and those who would need a lot of help.

Suddenly, I heard a whistle. A short man with curly blond hair and a light complexion called everyone to the middle of the field. This was Coach Stevenson. He was well mannered and seemed like a nice guy. He passed around a sheet and a few pens so we could officially sign up for the team. After we completed this administrative task, Coach made us run a few laps around the field next to the high school. It was usually used for football practice, but since football was a fall sport, our team could use it in the spring.

Most of the students knew each other. I only knew a few players, so I wasn't part of their conversations and jokes, but it felt good to be part of a team again. Once we finished running, Coach called the seniors together for a short pre-practice meeting. The rest of us grabbed soccer balls and waited.

"Noah, Snyder, Lars, and David, stand next to me," Coach shouted when he was done with his meeting. "Everyone else, form a line." I stood next to a big guy. He didn't look like your standard soccer player due to his size, but he seemed friendly. Then, Coach went down the line and counted us off, one through four. The number ones stood behind Noah, the twos behind Snyder, the threes behind Lars, and the fours behind David. This way, we were divided into four even teams.

"Teams one and two, to that field," Coach said, pointing to the field closest to the school. "Teams three and four, with me."

I was on team three, or "Team Lars." Lars was a Norwegian exchange student. He had come to the United States in August, so he had already made plenty of friends and was well adjusted to life in Mount Vernon. Lars had a thick accent, so I didn't understand him when he tried to speak to me. I asked him to slow down, which he immediately did. "Santiago, attack? Defense?"

I understood that. "Attack," I said.

"Okay. Up front, then," Lars responded, pointing to the forward position.

Fortunately, one doesn't need to say much to play soccer. If you can kick a soccer ball and have some idea about field positioning, you can communicate with signs and movements on the field. Soccer has its own "language."

At first, I was careful with the soccer ball and played it safe. Being the new guy, I didn't want to be flashy. I tried to observe and find out who the best players were. It didn't take me long to realize that Lars was the best player. I later learned that he had been part of the youth academy of Rosenborg, a famous Norwegian soccer club. No surprise there. He was good.

Another player who caught my attention was Adam Hall, one of our goalkeepers. Adam wasn't a tall guy, which is usually a requirement for his position. In fact, he was my height: around 5'10". He stood out because of his bleached blonde hair. He was athletic and had quick reflexes, but his footwork could use some work.

After a couple of hours, practice was over. It was a good first practice, and though it was a bit cold out, it helped to be running around. Before we left, Coach gathered all the players in the middle of the field to give a brief speech. I tried hard to understand what he said, but I missed most of it. I did gather two things, though: practice was every day after school, and we had a game on Saturday—against each other.

Wait, is that right? Our regular season was starting in two weeks, and we were going into it only getting to scrimmage against each other? This was the first year the high school had its own soccer team, so I was hoping we would play other teams in the pre-season to see where we stood. Unfortunately, it looked like that wasn't part of the plan.

We walked back to the locker room, and I picked up my backpack. Carrie was already waiting for me in the school parking lot. It had been a big day for me, and I was thrilled about it. I was finally making new friends, getting to play a sport I loved, and starting to adjust to my new home. Now, if only I could learn English faster.

Chapter Eleven
THE BEAUTIFUL GAME

April 10, 2000

After a couple weeks of practice, it was time for our first real game. I brought my old soccer cleats, shin guards, and a pair of sweatpants to school the day of the game. I also brought along some duct tape, which I planned to wrap around my cleats to cover my shoelaces. This had been my good-luck ritual when I ran track and field in Peru, so I decided to use it for soccer as well.

Our first official game was against Solon, another small school similar to Mount Vernon and located a short fifteen-minute drive away. Up until this year, our high school had combined with Solon's team, so many of our veteran players had played alongside Solon's in the past. I could tell our team was a bit nervous, but also hungry to win and excited about the opportunity to make a name for itself.

After an uneventful school day, the bell rang, signaling the end of classes. I grabbed my backpack from my locker and headed to the locker room. Noah, David, and Snyder were already there, and Coach Stevenson was passing out our uniforms. Snyder picked jersey number ten, and Lars took number eight. I was simply excited to get a jersey and ended up selecting number sixteen. That order of business done, we took a school bus to Solon.

I sat next to David on the bus, while Noah sat across the aisle with Lars. Both David and Noah pulled out portable CD players and some CDs from their bags for the ride. Seeing this, I took my fanny pack out of my backpack and put it around my waist, so I could listen to my Walkman.

"Santiago, what's that?" Noah asked.

"No way!" David said as he glanced over at me and started laughing uncontrollably.

"What?" I asked, surprised by their reactions.

They said a few words quickly that I didn't understand and pointed at my fanny pack. Something about the small storage device was extremely comical to them, and other students started coming over to see what was so funny. I didn't understand why they were laughing. Fanny packs were cool in Peru. Not only were they "in," but they were also expensive.

I quickly discovered that no one wore fanny packs in Iowa, as they had gone out of fashion a few years back. In fact, they had gone so far out of fashion that they were now objects of ridicule. Not surprisingly, my friends were making fun of my accessory.

To make matters worse, I didn't have a CD player like theirs in my fanny pack; I had a Sony Walkman that only played cassettes. Seeing this, David laughed even louder.

"Santiago, what is this? Do you come from the eighties?" Noah asked. I wanted to explain that my tape player was brand-new and that CD players were too expensive in Peru, so they weren't very popular. I grabbed my dictionary and searched for the correct words, but soon gave up. Explaining these concepts was just too complicated. I settled for saying, "In Peru, this is okay."

"That's fine, Santiago. It's okay here, too," Noah said, although I didn't believe him. He, David, and Snyder continued talking amongst themselves—probably about my electronics and fashion sense—so I turned on my Walkman and tuned them out.

I looked out the bus window and noticed that the weather hadn't changed much from the morning—still cloudy and rainy. It wasn't the ideal weather for soccer, as the ball tends to roll too quickly on wet grass. It was cold too, but at least it wasn't freezing cold outside anymore.

Within a few minutes, we arrived at Solon. It was still raining, so we changed on the bus. That's when I noticed that we had a following. Several cars had accompanied us from Mount Vernon, and about one hundred people were already sitting in the wet bleachers. There were plenty of umbrellas to go around.

Once we had changed, Coach said a few words, and then we jumped onto the field to warm up. We ran a few laps and some sprints and did some light stretching. With that, we were ready to play.

We all lined up, and the American national anthem came on the stadium speakers. This was unusual for me, since in South America, the national anthem is only played before the games of national soccer teams. I later discovered that, in the United States, the anthem is played before most high school games. I liked it, as it made the games feel more special and important.

I was soaking wet by the time the game started. We all were. The rain had only gotten worse as we warmed up, but people kept arriving at the stadium.

Although I could sense that most of my teammates were nervous, I wasn't. I tried to move around as much as possible so I could get open for a chance to score. I was the forward, and I knew that if I could get a good pass from Lars or Snyder, I could do some damage. Sure enough, only twelve minutes into the game, I received a pass from Lars. I took the ball, got past Solon's defenders, and shot it. The ball skipped in front of their goalkeeper and went in. Goal!

At that, everyone gathered around me, hugged me, and slapped my head. I wasn't sure why they slapped my head, but it was clearly a way to celebrate my goal. *If I score again, I'll have to cover my head. Otherwise, the team will slap me again*, I thought, bemused at this strange custom.

Five minutes later, Solon tied the game when one of their forwards took a deflection and shot it at goal. It went into the upper corner, which was impossible for our goalkeeper to protect.

The field was wet, and the ball went everywhere. It was hard to play. I tried to pass the ball around with Noah and Lars, but I kept missing my targets. I was relieved when it was halftime. I needed to refocus.

While Coach Stevenson gave instructions to the team, I jumped around, trying to stay warm.

For the second half, I knew I needed to change my strategy a bit. Since the ball had a mind of its own due to the rain, I needed to shoot at the goal more often. Then, we would see just what their goalkeeper could do.

Unfortunately, during the first part of the second half, things didn't change much. Both teams kicked the ball back and forth. Solon missed a few opportunities, and we didn't have a real chance to score.

Things changed fifteen minutes before the end of the game, though. A Solon player took David down outside of the box, and Lars got to take the free kick. His long kick was on-target, but Solon's goalkeeper deflected it. The ball bounced right in front of me, and I kicked it as hard as I could, scoring a goal. We were up again. I ran toward the bench to hug my team, and they all slapped my head again. *What is it with this kind of celebration? I might get a concussion the next time I score a goal*, I thought.

A few minutes later, I received a pass from Lars and took on four Solon players. I faked out a couple of them with a fancy move and ran past the other two. Once I was in front of the goalie, I gently placed it in the upper left corner. Goal!

This time, I ran toward the bleachers and celebrated with the fans, which were mostly parents and students. I didn't want to get slapped in the head again. A minute before the game ended, David passed the ball to me right outside the box, and I kicked it hard. The ball was wet, and it slipped past the goalkeeper's hands. I scored again.

We defeated Solon on their field in our first game of the season, 4-1. Everyone from Mount Vernon was thrilled. I didn't fully understand the fuss, as it was the first game of the season, but this game meant a lot to my teammates and coach, as well as to the families and students who came to watch. Having been combined with them in the past, Solon was our natural rival. It was the school we simply had to beat, and we had just done that.

We all hugged after the game, and then Coach said a few words as we rehydrated. It was no longer raining, but it was getting much colder, which meant that I had to change or at the very least find a warmer place.

Adam gave me a fist bump as we hurried back to the bus. Along the way, a skinny blonde girl approached us and said hi to him. It was apparent that they were good friends. Then, she turned to me and said, "Nice game, Santiago." I was taken completely by surprise. I had no idea how she knew my name, and I had never met her, yet she spoke to me as if we were old friends.

"Thank you," I said, trying to keep my cool. She smiled at me, hugged Adam, and walked to her car.

Adam noticed me blushing a little and started giving me a hard time. "Her name is Laura, and she's way out of your league, buddy," he said. Later that night, I learned the meaning of that phrase when I asked Heather about it at home. When I told her what had happened, Heather smiled and said that she agreed with Adam's assessment. I didn't.

As we lined up to get on the bus, more people came by to congratulate us. I heard my name a few more times and smiled. I had played soccer and run track back in Peru at a national level, but I had never received the amount or kind of attention I was experiencing now.

We finally got on the heated bus, and although we had just played in the cold rain for ninety minutes, our energy levels were high. I sat next to David and listened as everyone excitedly talked about different parts of the game. As we drove back to Mount Vernon, I thought about those weeks when I had felt depressed.

After all my doubts, fears, and loneliness, this was a wonderful day. I was now part of something. I was part of a team. I had friends. For the first time, I felt that I belonged to my new school.

Chapter Twelve
BROTHERLY ADVICE

April 13, 2000

I was home alone around six p.m. on a Thursday. Carrie had to pick Macy up from an event in Cedar Rapids, and Noah had given me a ride home after practice. Heather hadn't gotten home yet from visiting her cousin in town, and Edward worked the early night shift on Thursdays.

This past week at school had been different. After the soccer game, many students and teachers had started to recognize me. "Great game, Santiago," was something I had heard every day. I knew I had played well, but I still didn't understand the attention. We hadn't done anything significant yet. We had only won one game. However, just three weeks before, almost no one had even acknowledged me at school. I did like the difference.

While doing some homework at the kitchen table, I heard someone open the front door. James came in holding a newspaper. "*Eres famoso, hermano!*" he said as he threw the newspaper across the table. He was quite enthusiastic about telling me that I was now "famous."

"Why?" I asked.

In response, James opened the newspaper and showed me an article about the game. My name was all over it, and a picture of David chasing a ball appeared to the right of the article. I read it and was able to understand most of it. My English was getting better each day.

I asked James if we could speak in Spanish, as I wanted to have a fluent conversation with him. He nodded, so I launched into the tale of my past few days, explaining that I had received more attention in less than a week than I had in the past three months combined. I asked him whether this was due to the newspaper article.

"I figured you'd get attention. The newspaper will help spread the word, but that's not the main reason," James said.

"If it's not the article, what is it?"

"You're good at playing soccer."

I didn't think I was particularly good. I had played since I was a kid, so playing came naturally to me. "So?" I asked.

"So, that will get you attention. Americans love sports. We love athletes. Personally, I don't like the emphasis we place on sports, but that's just how we are."

"But what does that have to do with me? I'm not a professional athlete. I play soccer at a high school." I still struggled to understand why I was getting the kind of attention that only a professional athlete would get in Peru.

"Santiago, keep in mind that Iowa doesn't have professional sports teams. College and high school athletics are important here. Well, frankly, college and high school sports are important everywhere in America, but even more so in places like Iowa."

It took me a minute to fully process what James had said. Back in Arequipa, I had also been an athlete. Heck, I had accumulated plenty of track and field medals from running at national events, and I had played in several international soccer tournaments. But our teams rarely drew crowds as large as the one I had experienced a few days earlier at Solon. My family and friends rarely came to see my teams compete, even when most of our games were in the same city.

"Is it just with sports? Do other activities draw large crowds?" I asked James.

"Well, not really. Sports teams, especially football, bring large crowds. But people also go to theater and musical events."

"What about academic competitions?" I asked. In Arequipa, my high school participated in academic competitions, some of which were televised and received a lot of attention. I would think that a developed country like the United States would prioritize academic achievements over athletics.

"Not so much," James said, shaking his head, "at least, not as much as I would like."

"I see. That's unfortunate."

"It is." James loved to hunt, fish, and help out on his father's farm, but he was not planning to be a farmer. He enjoyed country music, riding tractors, and foraging for wild mushrooms, but he also enjoyed reading a good book. He believed in the importance of higher education and was attending Kirkwood Community College in Cedar Rapids at the time. He wanted to be a teacher, and he later succeeded in becoming one. He acknowledged the importance of sports in people's lives, but he wanted to see the same excitement for academic achievements.

I loved athletics, though. I had played soccer ever since I could remember, and I had run competitive track since I was twelve. This emphasis on sports wasn't a bad thing for me.

Sports had always been my way to make friends. Besides, even if people put too much emphasis on athletics, even a small school like Mount Vernon had excellent facilities to help anyone succeed in both sports and academics.

The school had a great library, which was much bigger than the library in my larger school in Peru. One classroom alone had more computers than all the classrooms in my Peruvian high school, combined. From what I could tell, most teachers were well prepared and cared about their students—although many of my teachers in Peru were just as good. Students in Mount Vernon ate a full lunch at school, not just a snack. They drove their own cars. They had heat in the winter. They had an opportunity to get a good education. I told James all of this and said that people should be thankful to grow up in a place like this.

"Sure, Santiago, we are blessed. I won't argue with you on that. The thing is, we're not competing with Peru. We're not even competing with Mexico or other Latin American countries. We're competing with China, Europe, and Russia. And we're being left behind. We need more scientists. We need to put more emphasis on academics," James explained.

I sat there in silence for a moment. I didn't know what to say. What had started with a simple question about sports was now a discussion about the flaws in the American educational system.

"Look, enjoy the fact that you can play soccer. You'll make a lot of friends. But as a former exchange student, let me give you some advice." James grabbed a piece of paper and a pen. He wrote three words: observe, compare, and share.

"First, observe. You'll be better off if you're aware of your surroundings and learn as much as you can from them. Also, not everyone will be nice to you. Most will, but many will want to see you fail. It comes with being good at something," James said as he circled the word *observe*.

"Second, don't compare. I can't stress this enough. You don't live in Peru anymore, so don't compare foods, places, or even people. I know it's hard to do. The food you eat here isn't 'like' something you ate in Peru. Get used to appreciating our food for what it is. You can compare things in your head, so you can process similarities and differences, but don't compare things in front of people. If you say that something is better in Peru than here, it can be annoying, or even offensive, to other people, especially to those who have never lived anywhere else." With that, James, wrote a big 'NO' over the word *compare*.

"Finally, share. You see the world with different eyes than most people you'll meet at Mount Vernon. You have a different perspective on it. Make sure people have the opportunity to learn from you. Share your experiences," he said as he circled the word *share*.

I thanked James for his candid advice and asked him if I could keep the piece of paper.

"Of course, Santiago. Any time," he replied.

I walked to my room and placed James's note inside my Anne Frank book. There was plenty of food for thought in that little note.

A few minutes later, I heard Carrie walk into the house. Macy knocked on my door and announced, "Santiago, we have pizza!"

I took off my sweatshirt and walked back out into the living room. Carrie, Macy, and James were choosing between taco pizza and supreme pizza. I grabbed a slice of supreme. This time, I didn't look for any silverware. I ate it with my hands.

Chapter Thirteen
DREAMS

April 14, 2000

Aside from small talk, I still couldn't say much in English. My reading and listening skills had improved a great deal, but my speaking skills were still below par. To help me with the learning process, Mr. Anderson had given me a grammar book, which I had been reading as much as possible. My Spanish-English dictionary was also getting plenty of use. In other words: I was trying, but I still wasn't fluent.

The main problem was that I hadn't learned English as a child, so when I arrived in Iowa, I mentally translated everything from English to Spanish and vice versa. My brain recognized the color blue and immediately thought of the word "*azul*," not the word "blue." Then, my brain had to translate "*azul*" to "blue." When someone said, "Hurry up," to me in English, I had to recognize those words first and then translate them into Spanish so I could process them. If I didn't understand an English word or phrase, I had to ask the other person to slow down or to repeat it.

Most students taking a foreign language during high school learn it that way: by translating back and forth. For me, it was frustrating, exhausting, and usually came with excruciating headaches.

It also led to peculiar conversations with strangers. For example, one night at the local grocery store, Carrie entrusted me with the task of finding evaporated milk. I couldn't find it on my own, so I approached an employee. "Hi, can you tell me where I can find evaporated milk?" I asked slowly and with a strong Spanish accent.

"What?" the employee responded.

I tried to enunciate better: "Evaporated milk."

"Oh, okay, evaporated milk," she said, rolling her eyes.

"Yes," I said, wondering why she had to be rude about it.

"Ail nain, botn' shel," she said, pointing at the other side of the store. I knew she hadn't meant to speak that gibberish, but that's what I heard.

"I'm sorry, slower please," I said.

She rolled her eyes again and said a few words under her breath. Then, enunciating every word slowly, she raised her voice and said, "AIL NAIN, BOTN' SHEL."

Nada. I didn't understand a single word she had said, so I remained standing in front of her in silence. She rolled her eyes once more, shook her head, muttered a few words under her breath again, and guided me to the evaporated milk. When we got there, I looked at the sign above the aisle and smiled. The employee had been saying, "Aisle nine, bottom shelf."

Moments like that happened often. When I told someone that I didn't understand and asked them to speak slowly, that person would raise his or her voice instead. I knew people were trying to be helpful, but raising one's voice wasn't the answer.

With time though, something strange started to happen. I wasn't sure if my brain was translating words faster, but I was beginning to understand English words much more quickly. I was beginning to think in English, and things were finally starting to "click." Some days were better than others, but for the most part, I could understand other people better.

I vividly remember the night when I woke up in the middle of it, sweating. I'd been in the middle of a dream in which my brother and mother were visiting me in Mount Vernon. I was showing them around the high school, the farm, and the town. We spoke in Spanish. Suddenly, Heather appeared in my dream, speaking in English. I introduced Heather to my mother, and they struck up a conversation. Heather would say something in English, and my mother would respond in Spanish. This bilingual conversation was rather strange and unexpected. In Peru, my dreams had, naturally, always been in Spanish. Although sometimes people had different accents, they all spoke in my native language. This was my first bilingual dream, and it bewildered me.

After this, the bilingual dreams continued. One beautiful April night, I had my first English-only dream. In that dream, I was playing soccer, and I was very vocal on the field. Although I used basic words, the conversations were solely in English. The next morning, I didn't wake up sweating. Instead, I smiled as I hadn't in a long time, hopeful that things would continue to turn around for the better.

Chapter Fourteen
THE LITTLE CALF

April 15, 2000

"Santiago!" Tom shouted as he pounded on my door with unusual force. "Hurry up! We don't have time to waste!"

Why is he desperately calling me? I wondered. It was still dark outside, and I felt unusually tired. I wondered what time it was, so I grabbed my watch. It was three in the morning. I could only imagine that it was an emergency.

The Novaks had to go out of town to pick up some cattle they had purchased from a farmer in northeastern Iowa. Heather and Macy were spending the weekend with friends, and James had to attend a school conference in Des Moines. My host parents thought I should spend the weekend with their neighbors, the Sedlaceks, so I wouldn't miss school in case their trip took longer than expected. I didn't mind staying with the Sedlaceks. In fact, I was excited about it, as they owned a few horses and had previously invited me over to ride with them. As a child, my father used to take me to a horserace track every weekend, and I had developed a fascination with riding horses.

Tom Sedlacek was a rugged, but kind, man whose grandparents had emigrated from the Czech Republic in the early 1900s. His wife, Camille, was a sweet and generous soul who had learned to put up with Tom's occasional stubbornness. They were farmers.

I quickly donned my jeans and a tee shirt and ran out of the guest room. Tom was wearing a thick coat and a hat. The coat hanger at their home contained seven or eight coats, most of which were "working" coats. There was also a bucket full of gloves, which were probably purchased at the local home improvement store. Next to that bucket was a pile of boots. There were four or five pairs of them, and most were caked with dirt.

"Come on, grab a coat. We need to help Camille. She's at the barn," Tom said as he opened the door. I grabbed whatever coat I could find and a pair of gloves.

"Should I call 911?" I muttered, as I didn't know what was happening.

As I ran to their barn, the wind slapped my face. It had been cold in Iowa that whole week, and the temperature hadn't even reached forty degrees Fahrenheit in five days. Technically, spring had started in late March, but on some days, it seemed that Iowa hadn't gotten the memo.

When I walked into the barn, Tom was already there, holding a bucket and locking some of the cows in what appeared to be a large cage. Camille was moving the remaining animals into a smaller room. One cow was lying on the ground.

"Santiago, come here!" Tom yelled as he ran to hold that cow's head.

"What do I do?" I said as I raced over, now fully awakened by the turmoil.

"Put your gloves on, quickly!"

I did so. "Okay, now what?"

"Pull the legs," he said. I looked at the cow and suddenly realized that it was giving birth, but was having issues with the delivery. This defied every single notion I'd ever had of living in the United States. I grew up watching American TV shows like *Saved by the Bell*, *Friends*, and *The Simpsons*, all dubbed into Spanish. None of these shows depicted life on a farm, let alone assisting a cow in giving birth.

In Peru, the closest I'd ever gotten to raising or even interacting with a farm animal was at my Aunt Emilia's home. Aunt Emilia lived in a beach house in Camaná, and she raised chickens for fun. When I was ten years old, my family spent a summer at her home. One day, she made me choose between two eggs. A few days later, I saw a little chick peck its way out of "my" egg. After seeing that miracle, I became attached to it.

I called my baby chick Paco. We became buddies that summer, and I fed him every day. When the summer was over, I had to say goodbye. I didn't see Paco for a few years, but witnessing his birth was an unforgettable experience. It was just as memorable as my next visit to Aunt Emilia four years later.

"Where's Paco?" I asked Emilia a few days into our visit.

"He's in a better place, Santiago," she said.

"What happened to him?"

Emilia looked at my parents as if she were asking for permission to continue. Whatever she saw on their faces prompted her to proceed, "Remember the dinner we had on Sunday?"

"Yes," I replied, unsure about what would follow.

"Well, Paco was a part of that," she said. I felt sick to my stomach. To think that we ate little Paco was traumatic and unsettling.

In addition to my lack of experience with farm animals, I was uncomfortable because the barn wasn't the cleanest place on the farm, especially when it was cold outside and the cows spent a lot of time in it. I tried not to step on any fresh manure and walked toward the struggling cow. I took a deep breath, grabbed the calf's legs sticking out of it, and pulled. The calf's legs were gooey, and I couldn't get it to budge. "Tom, this isn't working," I said.

He walked around the cow and came up with a different plan: he would hold the cow's hips, and Camille would grab its head while I pulled the calf's legs as hard as I could. "Once the calf is out, hold it," he said.

"Sure, if you put it that way," I mumbled. I grabbed the legs and pulled again. This time, I pushed my feet against a concrete slab. It worked. The calf started to come out.

As soon as the calf's head was out, the cow tried to stand up. Tom pushed it back down and asked me if the calf was breathing.

He has to be kidding, I thought. *I helped this cow give birth, and now I have to check to see if the calf is breathing?* I hoped he knew I hadn't gone to veterinarian school. I grabbed the calf's head and noticed that it wasn't breathing. It wasn't even moving. "It's not breathing!" I shouted.

"Crap!" Tom shouted as he pushed the cow into the nearby pen with the other cows. He ran to the calf, opened its mouth, and took a piece of sticky material out of it. Then he hit the calf on its side a few times until it began to breathe.

Camille brought over a towel and cleaned it. The calf was breathing, but we still needed to make sure that it would connect with its mother. Tom explained that it was possible that the cow might reject the calf and not feed it. We waited about thirty minutes until the calf was able to stand up by itself, and then we brought the cow and her calf together. The cow did the rest. She licked her calf's face, and the bonding process began.

We waited in the barn for another hour. I was tired, but I wanted to see what would happen to the little miracle calf. Unsurprisingly, nothing fascinating happened. I helped Tom and Camille clean up the mess we had made, and then Tom said we should go back to the house.

I walked back into the house around 5:30 a.m. I couldn't go back to sleep, so I took a warm shower and then waited in bed to observe the sunrise through the guest room window.

Could any other exchange student at Mount Vernon top this experience? I wondered. *Will people believe me when I tell them this story? I mean, I just pulled a calf out of a cow!*

Chapter Fifteen
THE SOLAR ECLIPSE

April 17, 2000

It was another spring afternoon in Iowa, and my soccer team had just finished playing a game against another school. It was another victory for our team. We were getting close to the end of the season, and we hadn't lost yet. This first year of soccer for Mount Vernon High School was turning out to be a great one.

The game had been a tough one, and our opponent school had a few players who were a bit violent. Apparently, they forgot that it was a soccer match and decided to play football instead. The unnecessary physicality wasn't new to me, but it got annoying. Usually, because I was a striker, I was the one taking the most punishment from players on the other teams.

In that game, however, this wasn't the case. Lars dribbled a bit more than usual in a few plays, and he paid for it: he ended the game with several scratches and a sore knee. In addition, it wasn't just the opposing players who picked on Lars—it was the opposing fans, too. As soon as he received the ball, a loud booing followed.

After the game, Lars and I walked back to the bus together. We had to walk across the soccer field, so we passed some students from the other school. This time, they more than booed Lars on our way to the bus—they insulted him while speaking with a heavy Norwegian accent, trying to mimic his. They crossed the line.

Lars muttered a response under his breath, calling them names, but they didn't hear him. I told him to let it go, as I didn't want things to escalate further.

Understandably, when we reached the bus, Lars was upset. "Where's Coach?" he asked Snyder.

"He's driving back with his wife today," Snyder responded. This meant that other than the assistant coach, we had no adult supervision on our way back home. The assistant coach was more like "one of the guys," as he was a student at the local college and helped our coach with practices a few times a week.

As we were getting ready to leave, those students who had insulted Lars walked toward our bus, since their cars were parked in the same parking lot. As they approached, one of the students put his hands to his mouth and went at it again. "Boo, boo, boo!" he yelled. Other students followed suit.

Lars, annoyed and frustrated, asked David to move out of his window seat. David immediately did so, and Lars jumped up onto it. Some of our fellow players started to laugh. Apparently, this wasn't the first time they had experienced Lars's erratic behavior. Lars opened the bus window and shouted, "Hey you," drawing the attention of the small group booing at him. Once they were all looking at the bus, Lars turned around, dropped his pants down to his knees, and showed those kids his pale rear end.

A loud laugh ensued from inside the bus. Some students brought their hands to their faces in disbelief, while some high-fived Lars. The younger ones didn't say much, fearing what the assistant coach would say. For his part, the assistant coach resorted to telling Lars to stop, but that was the extent of his involvement. I asked David whether he had seen Lars do that before. I had never seen anyone do such a thing in Peru.

"I haven't seen him moon anyone before, but I've heard he's been mooning around," he said with a grin.

"Mooning?" I asked. I grabbed my Spanish-English dictionary but couldn't find the word. Thinking I had misunderstood him, I asked David to look for the word in my small dictionary.

"Santiago, that word isn't in the dictionary. It's a slang term," he explained. *Slang?* That was also a new term, but I would have to get back to it later. I needed to understand this "mooning" business first.

"Mooning?" I asked again. "Can you spell it for me?"

"M-o-o-n-i-n-g. Like the moon in the sky," he said.

I smiled because when Lars had mooned those guys, the sun had hit my eyes, and for a split second, his rear end had covered the sun, like in a solar eclipse. "That was a solar eclipse of some kind," I whispered.

On the ride back to Mount Vernon, I thought about all the times at my Peruvian high school when my friends and I had misbehaved. It happened often, but it was mostly just innocent pranks. I couldn't recall a time when one of my friends had mooned students from another school. This was another first for me.

Chapter Sixteen
BURGERS, PIZZAS, AND BURRITOS

April 19, 2000

There were a few commonalities I noticed in many of the small Iowa towns I visited during my trips with the soccer team and my outings with my host family and friends. For instance, one could always find a small financial institution, which was a community bank, a credit union, or a small branch of a national bank. In these commercial facilities, tellers and personal bankers welcomed customers with a smile and a handshake. If a customer were a regular, bankers often knew them by name. Frankly, they often knew more than just the customer's name—they knew that customer's whole family history.

Each town also had a post office, which was likely located on Main Street. Many post offices had an extensive collection of commemorative stamps on their walls, which I found amusing. Most towns also had one or two gas stations, some modern, some not so much. Many had ice cream or soda shops, though I thought it would be hard to make a living selling ice cream during the long Iowa winters. The mid-sized towns had a couple of local boutiques and antique stores. They all had a few churches, which at the time, I described as the Catholic and the non-Catholic churches. All small towns also had a fire station and a police station, which provided a sense of safety and security to the communities they served. And of course, there were the dive bars; most towns had one or two of these establishments.

Many small towns even had at least one golf course, which I thought was impressive. My hometown in Peru, a city with over a million people, had one golf course, and it wasn't nearly as green and well-kept as the ones in Iowa.

Another unique feature of most small towns was the types of restaurants I encountered. There were at least four categories in each small town: Italian, American, Chinese, and Mexican.

By Italian, I mean either a locally owned place or a franchise like Pizza Hut. The menu included items like pizza, cheesy noodles, breadsticks, and lasagna. The décor was often comprised of an Italian flag here and there, a map of Italy, and perhaps a picture of a soccer team.

By American, I mean a local sports bar or a burger place like McDonald's or Burger King. Sports bars had two or three large TVs that were always tuned to a sports channel. These also featured beer on tap, chicken wings, burgers, fries, and perhaps some barbecue ribs. American flags, neon signs, oversized beer signs, and a picture of a football player or a team jersey would decorate these places. Some had a beat-up pool table.

By Chinese, I mean a locally owned restaurant or a China Wok. The menus included items like sesame chicken, General Tso's chicken, beef with broccoli, and egg drop soup. The decorations included some posters with what I assumed were Mandarin characters. A few local restaurants had a fish tank and pictures of Asian people on the walls.

And by Mexican, I mean a local restaurant with a Spanish name or a Taco Bell. The local restaurants usually offered chips and salsa as a free starter. If you were old enough, and I wasn't, most people would order a house margarita or a Mexican beer. Enchiladas, burritos, tacos, fajitas, beans, taco salads, guacamole, and cheese dip filled the menu. A few sombreros here and there, a Mexican flag, colorful signs, and paintings of typical Mexican churches completed the décor.

One standard feature of all these restaurants was that they usually had Spanish-speaking workers on staff. This meant that I could occasionally use my Spanish to order food or joke around with some of the restaurant employees.

*   *   *

One night, two guys I had met at a soccer party, Marcus and Jonathan, invited me to Tres Amigos, a local Mexican restaurant. They both played basketball, but they had gone to some of our soccer games. We had a lot of common friends, and we had gotten along well from the start, so they often gave me rides to the mall, to the movies, and really anywhere else I needed to go.

They brought their girlfriends, Sarah and Jennifer, along for our outing. Both girls were juniors at a neighboring school, though Marcus and Jonathan were seniors at Mount Vernon. Sarah, Marcus's girlfriend, had taken Spanish for three years, so she attempted to speak Spanish with me. It was funny because she only knew basic sentences, but she still tried to show off. Jennifer wasn't as outgoing. Unlike Sarah, she didn't have an interest in Spanish or in Mexican food. She was just tagging along because of Jonathan.

When we arrived at the restaurant, a short Mexican girl seated us. The restaurant had colorful walls, and it was decorated with what I assumed were traditional Mexican paintings. It wasn't a large place, but it was big enough that it needed four large TVs strategically placed in each corner. The TVs all played different soccer games.

A few minutes later, our waiter came over to take our drink orders. Another waiter brought a complimentary basket of chips and a couple bowls of salsa. This was unique to several of the restaurants I visited in the United States. Many Italian restaurants offered free bread, while some Chinese restaurants provided free egg rolls.

"Dig in," Sarah said happily. We all did, except for Jennifer. "Come on, Jennifer, have some," she added.

Jennifer didn't like Mexican food, and she didn't want to have any chips. Jonathan said she was a "picky eater," meaning that she would only eat chicken nuggets, French fries, some vegetables, and maybe the occasional burger. Maybe.

When the waiter came over and asked if we were ready to order, Jennifer chimed in, "Santiago, you go first. You probably know what's good here."

I didn't think much of her comment. I had noticed that our waiter spoke Spanish, so I asked her a few questions before ordering: "I always confuse enchiladas and burritos. What's the difference?" She explained the difference and gave me her recommendation, and I made my decision. "I'll have an enchilada, black beans, and rice, with lettuce and tomatoes on the side. No sour cream, please," I told the waiter in Spanish.

My friends loved it. They seemed sort of proud that I could speak Spanish so fluently. Sarah commented that she wanted to be able to speak like me. Marcus and Jonathan ordered tacos, and Sarah had some traditional Mexican dish I had never heard of before. Frankly, I didn't know much about any of the menu items, as Mexican food is so different from Peruvian food.

Then it was Jennifer's turn. "I'll have what Santiago ordered, but with chicken," she said. "He probably knows what's good here," she added.

Marcus turned to Sarah and rolled his eyes. Although Jennifer was Sarah's friend, Marcus clearly wasn't afraid to show that he didn't think much of her.

By the time the food came, the chips were almost gone. The plates were enormous—each dish could probably have fed three people. Marcus and Jonathan didn't waste any time and immediately started stuffing their faces with tacos.

"Marcus, babe, you're such a pig," Sarah said.

"Whatever. You love that about me," Marcus responded with a smirk.

"Gross," she added.

I just laughed. This wouldn't happen in my Peruvian house. My grandparents taught me to eat everything with a fork and knife, even fruit. Seeing my American friends eating tacos with their hands and not really caring about anyone else around them was funny to me.

"Santiago, I heard you like Laura Tomson. What's up with that?" Sarah casually said.

"What? Who said that?" I asked. Her question caught me by surprise. I didn't think I had ever said anything about liking Laura.

"I heard that you said she's pretty," Sarah added.

"Who said that?" I asked again. I mean, she definitely was pretty, but saying that I liked her wasn't accurate. I had barely exchanged more than a few words with her.

"Adam Hall, your goalie."

I remembered Adam asking me whether I thought Laura was pretty. I had answered affirmatively. But Adam had also told me that she was out of my league.

"You should ask her to prom," Sarah said enthusiastically.

I didn't respond, but I could feel my face getting warm. I was blushing.

"Leave the guy alone, Sarah. You're making him nervous," Marcus said, laughing.

"Fine. But I do think he should," she responded.

I hadn't really thought about prom. It was fast approaching, and I didn't have a date yet, but Laura? According to Adam, she wouldn't go out with me, and I trusted Adam. He had been a terrific friend to me.

"How's the food, Santiago?" Jennifer asked, changing the subject, which I welcomed. "I think it's pretty good, and I'm a picky eater."

"It's good," I said casually.

"Good? Or great?" she insisted.

I wondered what this girl wanted from me. She kept pushing for a firmer answer, but I wasn't sure why. I noticed the atmosphere at our table starting to get thick.

"I mean, you know, is it like food at home? Like your mom would make?" she finally asked.

I gave her a confused look as I tried to make sense of her questions, as they were factually wrong in two distinct ways. First of all, my mother didn't cook; our maid did. Second, I didn't eat Mexican food at home in Peru; I ate Peruvian food. In fact, the first time I ever had a taco was at a Taco Bell in Iowa.

"Well, no. I'm from Peru. I eat Peruvian food back home," I responded.

"Whatever. Same thing, you know what I mean?" she said.

I didn't. The two countries were geographically far apart and culturally and historically unique. And that extended to their cuisines. I wouldn't expect a Mexican citizen to know that a *pisco* sour is a delicious Peruvian drink or that *cuy chactao* is a Peruvian dish containing fried guinea pig. So why would Jennifer assume that my family ate burritos and enchiladas?

Sarah, Marcus, and Jonathan looked embarrassed and uncomfortable. They clearly thought her comments were offensive, and Sarah turned to her friend and said, "Jennifer, what are you doing? Why would you ask something like that?"

That's when I realized what was happening. Jennifer wasn't trying to be mean. She wasn't trying to be offensive at all. She just didn't know any better. Jennifer's contact with people from "south of the border" was very limited. She had grown up in a small town in Iowa, a state that is largely white. The Spanish teacher at her high school was from Mexico, and when the national media discussed issues related to South and Central American immigration, they talked about "immigrants coming from Mexico," lumping all nationalities into one basket. For her—and probably for many Americans living in the Midwest—if a person spoke Spanish, that person was probably from Mexico. She conflated Mexican culture with tacos, enchiladas, sombreros, and tequila. Of course, Mexican culture involves a lot more than that, but she didn't know it at the time.

For a moment, I thought about laughing at her comments and just letting them slide. But then I remembered what James had told me about sharing my experiences and my culture.

So that's exactly what I did. I didn't get upset, nor did I laugh. I used that opportunity to share more about my ethnic background. I told Jennifer more about Peru and what I knew about other cultures in Central and South America. I explained that I didn't understand what she meant about it being the "same thing" because all the countries "south of the border" are different. I mentioned that people in Argentina don't listen to *rancheras*, but they do dance to tango music; that people in Peru drink *pisco*, not tequila; that Mexico has a beautiful culture, but there's a lot more to it than what one could eat, drink, or see at a Mexican restaurant. I encouraged her to learn more about all Latin American cultures. To my surprise, she was very receptive. They all were.

On our way home, we listened to the punk band Blink-182 and didn't say much. Marcus and Sarah held hands and sang along to the music. Jonathan fell asleep, and Jennifer put her head on his shoulder. I looked out the window and thought about that night.

I felt that I had done something positive, something that my exchange program demanded of me. I had helped build a tiny bridge between our cultures. I had exposed my friends to something new. I had shared.

Chapter Seventeen
BROWN BOY IN WHITE AMERICA

April 20, 2000

The soccer season continued, and we played a few more games, all of them wins. I was enjoying my time with the team. My teammates had embraced me, and I'd made a few good friends.

This week, we were playing another undefeated team, this one from just outside Iowa City, a small city located twenty minutes south of Mount Vernon. Iowa City is the home of the University of Iowa, one of the three public universities in the state.

I loved Iowa City. Marcus had taken me there a few times to visit some of his friends who were in college, and they seemed to enjoy it. I especially appreciated that it was a college town, which meant it had an active downtown full of restaurants, study areas, coffee houses, and plenty of young, vibrant people.

College life in the United States seemed very different from college life in Peru, where students live with their parents or relatives during their university years. As Marcus explained it, "In the United States, once you graduate from high school and decide to attend college, you move into a dorm and live with hundreds of other students on the same college campus." That seemed like an exciting way to live while attending college.

This school we were playing was not a large Iowa City high school, but rather a small school, similar to Mount Vernon. Both schools were Class 1A, which is the classification for the smallest sports programs in the state. Still, when we arrived, I noticed that they had a large number of students already sitting in the bleachers. I thought this was a good sign, as thus far, our hardest games had been against teams with a good following. And I liked the competition.

As we warmed up, some fans from the other team sang a few songs, which wasn't unusual. But then, a couple of them shouted, "*Arriba, Arriba!*" I ignored them, but then they shouted this again a few minutes later, this time with a rather strong accent and rolling their r's excessively. I smiled, as I thought they were just making fun of my accent, which I knew was strong. They all burst out laughing.

"Don't pay attention to them," Snyder said.

"I won't," I said. Frankly, I didn't know why I would pay attention to those students or be bothered by their comments. If they wanted to get my attention because I spoke Spanish and had a strong accent, that was fine. I didn't care. Besides, I had a rule for myself: once the game started, I only cared about what my teammates and coaches said. I tuned everyone else out.

Fifteen minutes into the game, we were up 2-0. Lars had scored the first goal from a free kick, and Snyder had scored the second after heading the ball into the net after a cross. Up to that point, I hadn't had the best game, but it was because two players constantly marked me. Most teams in the area already knew that I had been scoring at least two goals per game, so they generally tried to rough me up a bit during the first twenty minutes. Once they realized that I didn't care about their plot and that I would get up every time, they would generally leave me alone. Especially after I scored on them.

Thirty-five minutes into the game, I took a pass from Lars and dribbled a couple of players, but I couldn't control the ball well, and it rolled away from me. I ran as fast as I could to recover it, and the goalkeeper came out of his small box to catch it before me. Luckily, I made it to the ball first and faked the goalie, but right as I tried to kick it into the net, he extended his right arm and grabbed my leg. I fell. The referee called it as a penalty kick. The other team's coach was furious, yelling that I had faked the fall. I hadn't. I didn't like players who faked fouls, so I never did it.

The referee handed me the ball. I walked to the penalty box and placed the ball on the penalty spot. I heard people yelling, but as usual, I tried to ignore them. This time, however, it was difficult, as some students had walked to the area behind the goal to heckle me. "Go back to Mexico!" one kid shouted.

Their goalkeeper walked toward me and tried to intimidate me. "Are you afraid now?" he asked. I didn't respond.

Some parents asked the referee to do something about those students, as no one is allowed to stand behind the goals. I'm not sure whether they had heard what the student said to me, but they wanted them out of there, which was fine by me. The referee stopped the game and ran to talk to Coach Stevenson and to the other team's coach. Meanwhile, the kids who had yelled at me ran away from the field after some parents went to confront them. It was chaos.

Lars grabbed my arm and pulled me to the side of the field. A few other players ran toward me and shielded me. Then, the referee walked over. "I'm sorry about this," he said. "Are you okay?"

"Yes, I'm fine," I said. Frankly, I didn't understand what was going on. I mean, I wasn't from Mexico, so their words simply didn't make sense. Also, why would that be offensive anyway? I had some Mexican friends, and they seemed like wonderful people. The whole thing was nonsense.

"Okay, then. Let's play," the referee said. Things seemed to calm down, and the game resumed. I grabbed the ball, set it on the penalty spot again, and took the shot. I scored and celebrated with my teammates.

A few minutes later, Coach took me out of the game. I had been playing full games until then, so his decision came as a surprise. "Are you okay?" he asked as I walked over.

"Yes, Coach," I responded, confused. Those students' comments didn't bother me or hurt me. They just didn't make sense to me.

I stayed on the sidelines for most of the second half. During that time, the other team scored a couple of times, and although we were still up 4-2, Coach wanted to make sure the game didn't get out of hand, so after a while, he called up a few of the regular starters to return to the game. "Santiago, get back in," Coach said. "If something happens, you tell me right away, and I'll take you out."

"Sure," I said.

Two minutes later, Lars passed the ball through a few players, and I sprinted toward it and kicked it. The goalie tried to block it, but it went through his hands. I scored again.

The game changed after that. It became much more physical, mostly against me. Every time I got the ball, I was tackled. Hard. As usual, I got up and kept playing. Coach was okay with my getting kicked here and there, but the game started to get out of hand.

On a corner kick, Lars grabbed the ball and got ready to take it. As I watched Lars kick the ball into play, another player punched me in the stomach. I dropped to the ground, and a brawl ensued. Lars came sprinting from the corner and pushed a guy who was trying to grab me. Snyder and Noah pulled me aside. Coach called Phil, who was warming up on the sidelines, to take my place.

The referee separated the players, and everyone calmed down. I was a player who got kicked a lot during games, but I usually remained calm. I just thought it came with the job. That hit was different though. It had a different tone, which was made crystal clear when Coach tried to take me out of the game again.

As I walked to the sideline to be substituted, a player from the other team, wearing number seven, walked toward me and grabbed my arm. "Leave. Go back to your country. You don't belong here," he said. He looked at me with a type of anger I had never experienced before. For the first time in my life, I was being discriminated against. I hadn't done anything wrong. I was just having fun with my high school friends. Yet I was being discriminated against because I was from a different country. Because I looked different. Because I was brown.

I looked at him and didn't respond. Instead, I ran toward my Coach. "Coach, please, can I finish the game? I'm fine," I said.

Coach looked at me and apparently realized that he should let me finish. He trusted me. He turned to the referee and made a change to the substitution. Phil was still going in, but for someone else.

There were ten minutes left in the game. I was tired, but I played the best soccer I could. We scored two more goals, one of which was mine. I was upset, and I felt a pain in my gut that I had never experienced before. I was mad. I didn't let that anger hold me back. Instead, I used it to my benefit. A couple of times, I intentionally took the ball to Number Seven's area of the field and dribbled right past him like he wasn't there. I made sure he would remember me, and he did.

When the game ended, the final score was 7-2 in our favor. It was a big win, and everyone celebrated. Everyone except me.

As usual, our team got together and walked over to the other team to congratulate each player. Although I didn't want to do it, I joined the team. Sure enough, there was Number Seven, ready to shake my hand. *Why should I shake the hand of someone who treated me that way on the field?* I thought. For just a moment, I thought about skipping him, but then I decided to just go through the motions and shake his hand anyway.

When I got to him, he grabbed my arm and looked straight into my eyes. "I'm sorry, man. I'm sorry for what I said," he said. His eyes were watery. It was a heartfelt apology. I nodded, accepted his apology, and walked away.

I didn't say much on the way home. Snyder noticed that I wasn't being myself and tried to cheer me up. "Forget about it, Santiago. They were jerks. We have your back no matter what," he said.

"Thank you," I responded softly.

That was the first time I had ever faced racial discrimination in my life. It hurt me. And for that, I will never forget it. Although it may appear minor to those who have faced discrimination all their lives, that moment was a significant one for me. It made me want to learn more about the history of racial and ethnic discrimination in the United States. It pushed me to learn more about my own identity.

Even though that game was one of my few negative experiences as an exchange student, I also experienced something special that day. I experienced the support of my many friends who understood that what happened wasn't only wrong, but that it shouldn't happen again. On that afternoon, I realized that being brown in the United States is like being stamped with a permanent mark on your body that makes you different. But I also realized that it's okay to be different. In fact, most people embraced me because of it.

On that day though, I also learned that not everyone did.

Chapter Eighteen
FIRE DRILLS

April 21, 2000

It was a school day, but Marcus, Jonathan, Adam, and I drove to the Cedar Rapids mall for lunch. The high school's teachers were having a meeting, so we had plenty of time to drive to the mall and back. Marcus and Jonathan also wanted to shop for new basketball shoes. Given that many schools in America had metal detectors and locked doors in 2000, it may sound strange that I was able to leave school for lunch. However, in small and safe Mount Vernon, parents could sign a document allowing students to leave the building for lunch. My host family had signed it for me, so all I had to do was show a pass to the security guard to temporarily leave school.

On our way to the mall, my friends were all teasing me. "Santiago, do you have a date for prom?" Marcus asked. They all had girlfriends, so they didn't have to worry about finding a date.

"No, not yet," I answered. Frankly, I hadn't planned on going, so I didn't see the need to ask anyone. Besides, prom was only a week away, and there weren't many girls left at the school that I could invite.

"What about Laura Tomson? What happened to that idea?" Jonathan asked.

"No way, that's not happening," Adam said, laughing.

I knew Laura was popular, but so what? If she didn't have a date, maybe I could ask her. "Why not?" I asked.

"Santiago, don't take this the wrong way, but she'll probably say no. You can ask her. I just don't want you to look like a fool when she says no," Adam responded.

Adam had previously told me that Laura was out of my league, and by now, I knew what he meant. Laura was smart, beautiful, athletic, and popular. In addition, some people said that her family was wealthy. While I was known as a good athlete in our school, I was still an exchange student from South America. I didn't have an aristocratic last name, my Peruvian parents didn't have college degrees, and I didn't come from a wealthy family. In fact, I was trying to save as much money as I could from my Rotary Club allowance so I could pay my parents back for my airplane tickets.

"Wait, does this mean that Laura Tomson doesn't have a date yet?" Marcus asked, clearly surprised.

"Nope," Adam said, shaking his head. Adam explained that her family had planned on being out of town on a vacation, but it had been canceled at the last minute, so now she would be in town for prom, but didn't have a date.

"So, Marcus, what do you think?" Adam asked. "Do you think we should encourage Santiago to make a fool of himself?"

"Let him drown," Marcus said, shrugging his shoulders. "Actually, Adam, why don't you ask Laura if she's interested?"

"Fine, I'll ask her when we get back to school. Is that cool, Santiago?" Adam asked.

"That's cool," I said in a relaxed manner.

Once we got to the mall, we grabbed lunch. Afterwards, Marcus and Jonathan shopped for sneakers, and Adam and I walked around some stores before heading back to Mount Vernon.

On our way back, Marcus and Jonathan were mumbling something to each other, so I didn't pay much attention. I was thinking about what I would say to Laura if she showed any interest in attending prom with me. I did notice, however, that instead of taking the interstate, Marcus took a gravel road back to town. Those roads, for the most part, didn't have much mid-day traffic. I sat in the back seat observing the scenery: endless Iowa farmland.

Suddenly, Marcus stopped in the middle of the road.

"Santiago, get out," Jonathan yelled.

I didn't understand why we needed to get out of the car. Meanwhile, everyone else laughed and made silly noises. We were in the middle of the road, and although I didn't feel that I should, I jumped out of the vehicle.

"Come on, Santiago, move!" Marcus shouted.

Where? Why? I thought.

Everyone else hopped out of the vehicle and ran around it, laughing uncontrollably. Once they circled the car and got back to their original spots, they all jumped back in. All except for me. I was too late. Marcus drove off, and they left me in the dust.

"Hey, stop the car!" I shouted. *What just happened?* I wondered. *We hadn't been in any danger, so what was the purpose of that?*

After a few seconds, Marcus stopped the car. I ran up to it, opened the backseat door, and climbed in. "What was that?" I asked.

"Newbie, it was a fire drill," Jonathan responded, "a Chinese fire drill." They all laughed again.

"You should've seen your face!" Adam said, pointing at me with one hand and covering his face with another.

A fire drill? A Chinese fire drill? What kind of twisted prank was that? I laughed so I wouldn't be the only one who wasn't, but I still didn't understand what had just happened.

They talked about it the entire way back to Mount Vernon. I rolled my eyes a few times. I thought the whole thing was ludicrous.

Once we got back to school, we walked to the cafeteria for study hall. Marcus, Jonathan, and I grabbed our backpacks and pulled some books out, but Adam said he had something to do in the library and that he would be back soon. He told the teacher monitoring study hall that he needed to get something from the library and got a pass to leave the cafeteria.

Snyder joined our table, and Marcus told him about our little adventure and how they had left me standing in the road. "You had to be there, Snyder. It was hilarious," Marcus assured him.

Very mature, guys, I thought.

Just then, Adam, who appeared to have been running, hurried over to our table. "Santiago, you need to go to the library. Now," he said.

"Why? What's up?" I asked. He seemed agitated.

"It's Laura," he said. "She'll go to prom with you, but you need to ask her right now. Someone else is about to invite her."

I tried to remain calm. "Okay. Where is she?"

"I just told you: in the library. Go now," Adam said. Although many students had study hall in the cafeteria, some had study hall in the library.

I stood up and headed to the library. This was my chance. I used Adam's technique and told the teacher that I needed to get a book from the library. Luckily, I got a pass.

The walk to the library seemed to last a long time, and a lot of things went through my mind during that time. What if Adam was kidding and this was just a prank? What if Laura wasn't even there?

When I got to the library, I noticed Laura sitting at a table by herself. I realized my palms were sweating. I rarely got nervous in front of other people, but I was a bit anxious now. "Hi, Laura. How are you?" I said with a thick Spanish accent.

"Oh, hi, Santiago. I'm good. What's up?" she responded cheerfully.

That was when I realized that I didn't have a plan. I just had to ask her. There was no time for small talk. "I wanted to ask you a question. Would you like to go to prom with me?" I probably sounded terrible. I was so nervous that I was shaking.

"I'd love to," she said with a big smile. I couldn't believe it: she'd said yes.

"Okay, great. I'll call you," I said and walked out of the library. And that was the end of our awkward, but productive, exchange. It didn't matter, though. I had a prom date, and it was Laura Tomson. I walked back to the cafeteria with a massive smile on my face.

"So, what happened?" Adam asked.

"She said yes."

Without hesitation, Marcus and Adam stood up and started applauding. Soon, everyone in the cafeteria was clapping. Most of them didn't know why, but they followed my friends' lead. The study hall monitor asked everyone to sit down and be quiet, although it was already too late: I was already embarrassed. My face was red as a tomato.

A few minutes later, I realized that I had told Laura that I would call her. But how? That was probably the third time I had ever spoken to her. "Hey Adam, can I ask you something?"

"Sure, man."

"After I asked Laura to prom, I said that I would call her."

"You don't have her number, do you?" he said, laughing.

"No, do you?" I asked.

"No worries, Santiago, I got your back," he said. He seemed to be proud of me.

I certainly was. This Peruvian boy had a date for prom.

Chapter Nineteen
MY AMERICAN PROM

April 29, 2000

I didn't have anything to wear to prom, so I asked my host family for help. Carrie said she would take me to a clothing store to rent a tuxedo for the night. I had never worn a tux before, but it was an important occasion: my first and only prom in the United States.

We drove to Cedar Rapids and parked in front of a fancy clothing store. As soon as we walked in, a well-dressed lady welcomed us, and after we explained my predicament, she helped us through the process. The lady took my measurements and entered them in a computer. "Please wait here," she said and then disappeared into a back room.

Carrie and I roamed the store while we waited, looking at the hundreds of shirts and coats available. I was shocked by the staggering amount of fancy clothing around me. After a few minutes, the lady returned with a tuxedo draped over one arm, and she escorted me to the dressing room.

I tried on the tuxedo, and it was a perfect fit. It looked as though it had been made for me. I didn't know how to put on the bow tie, but the lady helped me with it and also with my belt, which wasn't a regular belt.

"You won't believe this, but this tux fits him perfectly," the lady said to Carrie as I studied my appearance in the mirror. "It's on sale, too. It's a bargain, really."

"Perfect! No alterations," Carrie said. I didn't understand Carrie's excitement, but I later learned that alterations can make fancy clothing even more expensive. "So how much is it?"

"Let me see." The lady pulled out her calculator and did some math. "With taxes, it's $101.99."

"One hundred dollars?" I asked Carrie, opening my eyes as if a horse had stepped on me. *And this is on sale?*

"Yes. Pretty expensive, huh?" she said.

No kidding. Although I had grown up in a middle-class family in Peru, the exchange rate wasn't kind to Peruvians. One dollar was worth 3.50 *soles*, the Peruvian currency. My family made money in *soles*, so their buying power was severely reduced when dealing with goods priced in dollars. To put things in perspective, in 2000, the minimum wage in Iowa was about $5.15 per hour, or about $893 per month for an individual working forty hours per week. The median income for an Iowa household was about $41,000 per year. By contrast, in 2000, the minimum wage for an individual in Peru was about 410 *soles* per day, or about $117 per month. And unlike the median household income in Iowa, which was higher than the minimum wage, the median income for Peruvian families didn't differ much from their minimum wage. In any event, my little Iowa tuxedo was going to cost me almost the same as the monthly minimum wage for a Peruvian worker.

Carrie wanted to pay for my tuxedo, but I wouldn't let her. The Novaks had been so kind to me thus far, and I didn't want them to pay for this. She had accidentally left her wallet in the car, so while she walked out to get it, I took the single hundred-dollar bill out of my wallet and added all the coins I had in my pocket. Since I didn't have a credit card, this money represented my entire monthly allowance from the exchange program.

I was short a few cents, but the lady at the store noticed what I was trying to do. She picked up the money I had put down, said "Thank you," and gave me my tuxedo along with a receipt. I thanked her as well. I walked out of the store just as Carrie was coming back in and told her that I had already paid for the tuxedo. She got a bit upset and informed me that she would pay for the flowers, no questions asked. I agreed.

*   *   *

It seemed that the Novaks and the Tomsons had spoken about the prom arrangements in advance, because Carrie knew the details of our plans even before I did. Laura would pick me up from the Novaks' place at five p.m. and drive me to her house to meet her family and take pictures. After that, she would drive us to an Italian restaurant in Iowa City, for which we already had reservations. Following dinner, Laura would drive us to prom. She wouldn't drive me home afterwards, though. Instead, Mark Pitlik, a friend of the Novaks who was also in one of my classes and lived close to my host family's farm, had offered to drive me home after prom. Laura wasn't the best driver, so she had planned to spend the night at a girlfriend's house in Mount Vernon.

The day of prom, she arrived at the Novaks' home a few minutes early. Laura and I were about the same height, so I was surprised that she was wearing heels and had a high up-do. Although she looked like a princess, she was a very tall princess. Carrie took a picture of us, and it was an extremely awkward photo. Not only was Laura taller than me in her heels, but I didn't know how to stand next to her. Since she wasn't my girlfriend, I didn't feel comfortable holding her hand or hugging. Instead, I stood next to her and crossed my hands in front of me. She did the same. We were the perfect portrait of two awkward teenagers.

After some small talk, we were on our way. Laura drove a fancy SUV. I had never ridden in a vehicle that new or, well, that expensive. She had a reputation for being a questionable driver, so I was a bit uneasy, especially when we passed a couple riding their bicycles on the two-lane road. Laura drove over into the other lane to give the cyclists ample room, not realizing that another vehicle was fast approaching in the opposite direction. She had to swerve back to our lane to avoid a collision.

After a few minutes of driving on that paved road, Laura turned onto a gravel road. Unlike most of the main roads in Iowa, which are surrounded by agricultural fields, this road was surrounded by what appeared to be a small forest. Her home was in the middle of it. It was one of the most beautiful homes I had ever seen in my life. We walked into her house, and her parents were already waiting for us. We took more awkward pictures in their living room and their library. I was nervous, so I didn't say much. I just smiled a lot.

As we posed and smiled in this beautiful house, I couldn't help but think about the fact that, just a few days earlier, I had been discriminated against due to the color of my skin and my country of origin. Laura's parents met me for the first time that day, but unlike the hostile strangers at the soccer game, they were genuinely open and kind. They made me feel welcome in their home. Why the difference? And most importantly, why was I thinking about the color of my skin at that very moment? Such thoughts had never occurred to me before, so why now?

After we finished taking pictures, we exchanged hugs and said goodbye. On our way to Iowa City, I tried to tell Laura a little more about myself, but I was still nervous, and I couldn't articulate my thoughts clearly. She seemed to be okay with that, though. She was clearly excited, as was I.

The drive to the restaurant only took a few minutes. Once we were seated at our table, the server brought us the menu. It was a fancy restaurant, and the main dishes were expensive. I had brought a fifty-dollar bill, thinking that our meal wouldn't go over that amount. I couldn't afford much more anyway, as the tuxedo had made a significant dent in my savings. Unfortunately, no entrée was priced below thirty dollars.

Laura noticed that I kept looking at the prices and told me not to worry about it. She would pay for our meal. Well, her parents would pay for it. I wanted to insist on paying, but the math just didn't add up. I couldn't afford to. I could barely afford my own meal. Although I went along with her on this, I was deeply embarrassed.

We both ordered spaghetti with red sauce. Frankly, I just ordered the same thing Laura did because I didn't want to order something more expensive than she did. After the food came to the table, I realized that this was a poor choice. Eating spaghetti with red sauce while wearing a tuxedo and a white shirt is not a good idea. I usually didn't have any problems with spaghetti, but I was clumsy with nerves. I was two bites in when Laura brought her hands to her face in horror. She pointed at my shirt and handed me a napkin. I had managed to splash red sauce on my white shirt.

I excused myself and walked to the bathroom. There, I took off my coat, vest, and shirt and tried to wash the stain off the shirt with some soap. Then I dried my shirt with paper towels and the air dryer. I put everything back on and was out the door in less than five minutes. Laura noticed I had washed my shirt and laughed. After a couple of hours of being together, we had finally broken the ice.

Mount Vernon's prom was held at the school itself, and on our way there, Laura and I finally got to talk a bit more. Although to most people, she was "Laura Tomson," a popular and somewhat unreachable young woman, I discovered that she was actually a sweet, down-to-earth, and kind person. She seemed to be an old soul, and we enjoyed each other's company.

Prom itself wasn't what I had expected at all. In fact, "prom with Laura" ended a few minutes after we entered the building. We walked inside together, took the official prom picture, and then we separated. I had hoped to dance with her and get to know her better, but that didn't happen. Laura and I spent more time with our friends than with each other.

At first, only a few students were dancing, but after a few songs, most joined in. I noticed that except for the few slow songs, most students didn't dance as a couple with their date, but rather in large groups. I was not used to that, as most of the dances I had attended in Peru involved salsa dancing, which is generally done as a couple. I can't exactly recall all of the music played at my American prom, but I can tell you that it was not salsa.

Just before prom ended at midnight, Laura came over to me, gave me a hug, and thanked me for inviting her. We took a picture with my friends, and then she left with hers. I had barely spent any time with her.

My Peruvian prom the year before had been very different. I wore a suit rather than a tuxedo. Since I went to an all-male school, I invited a friend from another school. My parents drove me to my date's home, where I met her parents and gave her an orchid corsage. She wore an elegant coral-colored dress. Then, my parents drove us to the school auditorium. Yes, in Peru, the parents attend prom with their children. They get all dressed up, just like us. Dinner was served in the elegantly decorated auditorium as part of prom, and the parents had dinner with the students. I had my "first dance" with my mother, and even though eighteen is the legal drinking age in Peru, I had a drink with my father. The parents left around eleven p.m., and then a local band started playing Latin music for us "kids." The band played salsa, merengue, and other Latin dances for a couple of hours, and then a DJ played more Latin music until six a.m. I danced until my feet hurt. We all did. No one was allowed to leave the auditorium, and no one did. My parents picked us up for breakfast when prom ended in the morning. Only after we'd had breakfast was it time to go home.

If my Iowa prom had been different, my after-party experience was completely unexpected. After prom ended, Mark, who was with a group of people I didn't know, asked if I was ready to leave. Since I was not planning to attend the official after-prom party in the school gymnasium, I hadn't brought any clothes to change into, as most people had. "Sure, let's go," I said, thinking that he would take me home.

"Want to go to an after-party? It's out by my house," he said.

I hesitated because the original plan had been to have Mark take me home after prom. After a moment though, I agreed, thinking that it would be a small, harmless gathering. We walked to the parking lot, and three cars full of people were waiting for us.

"Santiago!" a girl shouted from one of the cars. I didn't know who she was, but she asked me to get into her car, which was full of girls in revealing tops and tight jeans. Based on the clothes they wore, they clearly had not attended our prom. Mark said it was okay, that her name was Kaleigh, that she attended another school, and that she was going to the party as well. I was unsure about the prospect of riding with a group of high school girls I didn't know, even though they seemed harmless, but I felt better when Mark said he would meet me at the party. With that, he jumped in another car and left.

I walked over to Kaleigh's car, and a girl opened the backseat door for me. As I sat down and closed the door, I noticed some smoke coming from the front seat and quickly recognized the distinct smell: a strong mixture of alcohol and marijuana. I should have jumped out of the vehicle right then, but I felt that I had no other choice but to ride with them. Mark and Laura had already left. My host sister, who also attended prom, had left as well, and I didn't want to bother my host family. Besides, how would I call home? I didn't have a cell phone, and the school didn't have a pay phone.

I'm sure I could have found someone to help me, but everything happened too quickly.

The ride to the party was a bumpy one. The party was out in the country, so our drive was on gravel roads. To make matters worse, Kaleigh had been drinking, and it was apparent in her driving. Although we drove in the direction of my host parents' home, Kaleigh turned onto another road about a mile from it.

"Where are we going?" I asked the girl sitting next to me.

"To 'The Farm,'" she responded calmly. I knew we were going to *a* farm, as Mark lived in the countryside, but which farm? What I didn't know was that we were going to a place commonly known by some students as "The Farm," which was actually an abandoned wooden gazebo surrounded by trees in the middle of a farm owned by an absentee landowner. It served as the perfect party spot for high school students in the area.

"We're here," Kaleigh announced when we pulled up. Dozens of kids were meandering around the gazebo. Many of them held beer cans, some clutched cigarettes, and others were smoking marijuana. I didn't recognize anyone. They all seemed to be students from a different school. I walked around in circles looking for Mark, but I couldn't find him. I became especially concerned when some of the students started to build random bonfires. *Alcohol, cigarettes, marijuana, and now fire?* This night wasn't looking good for me. In fact, it didn't look good for any of us.

"Kaleigh, could you take me home?" I asked after awhile. She noticed my desperation and told me to calm down, assuring me that Mark would appear at any minute. It had been about an hour since we left the school, and Mark hadn't arrived, so it was fair to assume that he wouldn't come. In fact, he never showed up at all. I didn't ask Kaleigh to take me home again. She was too drunk to drive anyway.

I looked around for someone who seemed sober enough to start a conversation. I needed to find someone, anyone, who could drive me home. It was dark, and the smoke from the bonfires began to cover the area. This meant that the "hidden" party would soon be noticeable from a distance. *Noticeable to the police*, I thought.

Then, suddenly, a girl walked toward me and grabbed my hand. "Santiago, you need to leave," she said urgently. I recognized her: it was Toni, one of the students in my Spanish class. Her watery eyes told me that she had been crying.

"I know. Could you take me home?" I asked.

"Yes, but we need to leave right now," Toni said, wiping some tears from her face. I asked if she was okay, and she said that she wasn't. As we drove away from the party, she explained that she had gone to prom that night with her boyfriend from another school. They'd had a fight during prom, and he left in a huff. Afterwards, one of Toni's friends told her that her boyfriend had driven to The Farm, so she drove there to talk to him. Unfortunately, she found her boyfriend kissing another girl. Toni was a good girl. She deserved better. After she saw her boyfriend with another girl, she wanted to leave The Farm without making a fuss. That's when she saw me wandering around. "This place is nothing but trouble," Toni said.

She was right. The following day, I found out that the police had showed up a few minutes after we left. Many partygoers were cited for underage drinking. Some even had to spend the night in the hospital, as they were extremely intoxicated.

Once I got home, I went straight to my room. It had been an emotional night. One thing was clear, though: I had to be more careful. I had to make sure I wouldn't put myself in a situation where I could end up in the wrong place at the wrong time.

Before going to bed, I thought about my time with Laura. Although it had been a good date, I couldn't stop thinking about how she had noticed that I was concerned about the restaurant bill. How she realized that I couldn't afford a meal at that fancy Italian restaurant, which was one of her family favorites. I realized that even though we went to the same high school, we lived very different lives. *Someday I'll be able to afford a place like that*, I thought.

Chapter Twenty
TOILET PAPER

May 20, 2000

In Arequipa, my high school class was known for its pranks. We terrorized teachers with our mischief, and even today, about twenty years later, students still talk about our antics. We turned all the desks in our classroom around to face the wrong way before teachers came into class—in Peru, teachers don't have their own classroom and have to move from classroom to classroom after every bell. Some students would simulate the sound that a 3.0 earthquake would make by hitting the concrete walls. Since earthquakes are common in Peru, and especially in my hometown, most teachers fell for it. We even started a small bonfire in one of our classrooms at the end of our senior year. No one got hurt, but we got in a lot of trouble for it. As punishment, the perpetrators were not allowed to attend our high school graduation ceremony. Although I was able to attend because I did not participate in building the fire, not seeing my friends attend our ceremony was the lowest point of my high school experience. In short, we caused a lot of trouble. Something good came out of it though: years later, many of my friends from my high school class still get together on a weekly basis, and those pranks had a lot to do with making that happen. We have a bond that is difficult to break, even when I haven't seen many of these people in years.

At Mount Vernon, because I enrolled in January and my exchange program was for the entire calendar year, I entered as a junior in the spring of 2000 and didn't have to participate in the graduation ceremony at the end of the school year. In fact, I never even got a diploma from the school.

Although I didn't attend Mount Vernon's graduation ceremony, I did observe some of the graduation rituals, starting with Snyder's graduation party. He was one of the few graduating seniors from my soccer team, and I was excited to celebrate with him.

The day of his graduation party, Carrie dropped me off at Snyder's house in town in the mid-afternoon. I planned to stay with David's family that night, as he lived just a few blocks away from Snyder. All throughout the party, people came and went from his house. They all congratulated Snyder and his parents, but he clearly didn't like the attention. In many ways, it felt like the party was more for his parents than for him.

The highlight of the event happened around five p.m.: Snyder had to speak and thank everyone for attending his party. Even though he wasn't considered a great speaker, he managed to mumble his way through a somewhat-decent speech. After that, most of the parents left, and only his friends remained at the house.

We played a soccer video game on his Play Station, and though I didn't usually enjoy video games, I joined in. As I expected I would, I finished dead-last in the tournament-style game we played. For snacks, Snyder's parents made "pigs in a blanket," which are hot dogs wrapped in crescent rolls and baked. They looked like fingers, but I enjoyed them.

Around 9:30 p.m., David asked if I was ready to go. It seemed a bit early to leave, especially since it was the weekend and David only lived four blocks away, but I agreed. We said goodbye to Snyder's parents and thanked them for their hospitality. Snyder walked us out and gave us a hard time about leaving early. I later learned that it was all part of a plan.

Once we got to David's house, we said hello to his parents and then headed to his room. There, he closed the door, pulled out a map of downtown Mount Vernon, and explained that we would actually be heading back out in a couple of hours for a surprise. With that, he laid out the plan for me: we would meet a couple of guys at Noah's place, which was just a few blocks away, thirty minutes before midnight. Then, we would walk to Snyder's place to drop off "a present." David asked if I wanted to help.

"Sure, I'll help," I said. I thought it would be fun to get together and surprise Snyder. I didn't know what the surprise present was, but I wanted to help out.

We left David's home a little after eleven p.m. David's parents had left the house a little earlier to attend a birthday party in Cedar Rapids, but they knew we would be out while they were gone. It was graduation weekend, and we had told them that we would be going to different houses around the block.

When we arrived at Noah's, I saw that Lars and Adam were also there. Noah asked us to help him take the "present" out of the trunk of his car. I opened the trunk and found two large containers. "What's in here?" I asked.

"You'll see very soon," Noah said, laughing. I picked up one of the containers, expecting it to be heavy, but it wasn't. It was rather light. "Let's go. It's time," Noah said to the group. We all followed him, with Lars and I carrying the two containers. Apparently, the exchange students were in charge of the precious cargo.

We stopped about fifty feet from Snyder's home, and Noah explained the plan: "Okay, guys. Once I say 'go,' grab two or three rolls and run to the front of Snyder's house. Throw them at the big tree in the front yard. We have to do this quickly."

What rolls? What is he talking about? What are we throwing at the tree? I opened the container. It had about ten rolls of toilet paper inside. "Wait, we're throwing toilet paper?" I asked David, confused.

"Yes, sir," he said with a grin.

"Aren't we going to get in trouble for this?"

"Nah, it's something we do. Don't worry."

Adam was the first to walk up to Snyder's place. He needed to make sure Snyder's lights were off before we could get started. Noah and Adam remained in contact on their cell phones. They talked for a minute, and then Adam gave us the okay. "Let's go!" Noah ordered.

With that, we all grabbed two or three rolls of toilet paper and ran to Snyder's place. Once we arrived, we threw the toilet paper at the big tree in front of his house. I knew this was wrong, but it was fun. I was probably breaking the law, but it felt great to be part of a group, to be a bit mischievous.

Just a few minutes later, a light came on inside. We took off running as fast as we could.

When we got back to Noah's home, we dashed into his garage and couldn't stop laughing. The adrenaline was still flowing, and we all high-fived each other. It was exciting. Silly, probably illegal, but fun.

The next day, David's parents got a call from Snyder's father. I had a feeling that we were in trouble. I mean, how did we think we could get away with something like this in such a small town? Apparently, we didn't. The neighbors recognized a few of us when we ran away.

"Alright boys, get up," David's father said, coming into David's room. "You have some cleaning to do this morning."

"What are you talking about, Dad?" David asked, playing the innocent card.

"David, get up. I'm not going to repeat myself. Snyder's parents are waiting for you two." David's dad was a former Marine, so we didn't mess around with him.

"Okay, sir," David said.

We walked to Snyder's place. Noah and Lars were already there, and we noticed that Snyder's parents had put three or four chairs outside in front of the beautifully decorated tree. "Welcome, boys," Snyder's father said. "Go grab a stick and a bag."

Snyder came out of the house and walked toward us. "Idiots," he muttered. We laughed quietly. We didn't want to get into more trouble.

It had taken us just a few minutes to make the mess and about three hours to clean it up. It was my first—and last—toilet papering experience. It was nonsense, and we could have been in a lot more trouble. Good thing my friend's parents had a sense of humor.

And what were the chairs for? Well, David's and Noah's parents came to watch. The chairs were for them, and they got to enjoy some parental bonding time while we cleaned up our mess.

Chapter Twenty-One
A FOX IN ITS CAGE

May 23, 2000

I have always been interested in politics and current events. Growing up in a country like Peru, where political events impacted people's everyday lives, it was hard *not* to have political opinions.

In the mid-1980s, a young Alan Garcia won the presidency by charmingly advocating for change through well-crafted and hypnotizing speeches. Unfortunately, this inexperienced president—he was only thirty-six years old when he took office—drove Peru into the worst depression of its modern history. His government was marked by hyperinflation. To put it into perspective, the average American inflation per year is about three percent, give or take. Peru's annual inflation when Garcia left office was over two thousand percent, terribly destabilizing the Peruvian economy.

Then, from the mid-1980s through the mid-1990s, the Shining Path and the Tupac Amaru Revolutionary Movement (MRTA) terrorized my homeland. In ten years, these terrorist organizations killed over seventy thousand people combined. Both organizations sought political and social change. MRTA's motive was to establish a socialist state, while the Shining Path followed a stricter communist ideology. Both organizations used violence and destruction to achieve their goals.

On top of that, in the mid-1990s, Peru had a military conflict with Ecuador, which claimed the lives of hundreds of people. For my generation, growing up in Peru was not easy.

So when I moved to Iowa, I wanted to learn more about American politics—not just from books, but from talking with the locals. I wanted to immerse myself in current events and learn from the world's "best."

In Mount Vernon, I became acquainted with Mike and Jenny Martin. The Martins were what one would call a rural middle-class family. Mike had graduated from Iowa State University with an agricultural degree, and Jenny had a degree in communications from a small private Iowa college. They met at a wedding. He was a friend of the bride, and she was the groom's sister. They claimed it was love at first sight.

From a young age, Mike knew he would work on his family's farm. The community had a lot of respect for his father, whom he called "Pops." His father owned several acres of land, which he had purchased over time through hard work and a bit of good luck. Unfortunately, that good luck ended when, at the young age of fifty-two, he was diagnosed with liver cancer.

When Mike found out, it was already too late. His father didn't tell anyone about his diagnosis until the day he collapsed at the farm. Mike had been working with his father that day. He saw his father stop his tractor, take a few steps out into the field, and fall. Mike ran to help him and found his father unconscious. He rolled him onto his back and ran to his parents' home. His mother, who had been in the kitchen making lunch for them, ran out of the house to help, while Mike called 911.

Mike's father spent a couple of days in the hospital, but it was the news the doctor delivered that was truly devastating: the cancer had spread, and there wasn't anything they could do. Mike's father died a few weeks later. From that day on, Mike, an only child, took care of the family farm.

As for Jenny, she had moved to California after high school to pursue her dream of becoming an actress. Unfortunately, she got involved with the wrong crowd, and trouble ensued. After two years of barely being able to make ends meet, she left her dream in California. She moved back to Mount Vernon and lived with her parents for a few months before entering a local community college. Although she had a rocky start, she turned her life around, transferred to a four-year college, and graduated with honors.

After they got married, Mike built a house for Jenny. Her childhood dream had been to one day live in a house with a white picket fence in Hollywood. California wasn't in Mike's plans, but he still wanted Jenny to have her dream home, even if it was in the middle of an Iowa farm. So he built it, right next to a stable that his father had built when Mike was young.

Mike worked on the farm, and Jenny worked at the local community bank. They had two kids, both of whom were in college when I met them. Neither of them wanted to work on the farm. The younger generation's lack of interest in farming is a real problem for Iowa farms and farmers. Young people prefer to move to larger towns and cities, where they can find more lucrative opportunities.

Politically, the Martins used to be "middle of the road," as they put it. But after Bill Clinton became president in 1993, they began to sympathize with the Republican Party. They didn't agree with many of the Clinton administration's decisions, and by the time the Monica Lewinsky scandal came along, they could no longer see eye-to-eye with the Democrats.

The Martins weren't unique in this. Many people living in rural communities in Iowa are Republicans and don't agree with the core beliefs of the Democratic Party. At the time of my exchange program, many believed that the Democrats were digging the country into a deep economic hole and that something needed to change. Many despised President Clinton's behavior, and the image of him lying to the American people after the Lewinsky scandal was all they could focus on. Some even said that the country would cease to exist if a Republican wasn't elected soon. I thought that was a bit extreme.

This dislike for the Clinton administration was extremely confusing for me. In Peru, during the 1990s, the United States was viewed as a beacon of freedom and prosperity, and this was mainly attributed to the actions of the Clinton administration. Yet for many Republicans, "Armageddon" was just around the corner.

What was I missing? Was President Clinton truly the worst president in the history of the United States, as many Republicans claimed at the time? I needed to know more, so I did what many people didn't do at the time: I listened.

*   *   *

Mike and Jenny invited me to dinner one night. They wanted me to try their favorite restaurant in Cedar Rapids. They'd had me over for dinner at their home before and had been meaning to take me to their favorite spot. That afternoon, Carrie dropped me off at the Martins' farmhouse a little earlier than planned, and Mike and Jenny weren't ready yet. Mike asked me to wait for them in the living room for a few minutes. I decided to turn on CNN while I waited. They were discussing the upcoming presidential election.

When Mike came downstairs, he saw what I was watching and said, "Santiago, please turn that off."

"Why?" I asked, honestly surprised.

"Because they're a bunch of liberals. You don't want to fill your head with that," Mike responded. "Liberals" was a word that clearly had a negative connotation in the Martins' home, but I didn't know what it meant.

Up to that point, CNN *en Español* had been my primary source of American news in Peru. I had never even considered the possibility that they were biased. If anything, I always thought that the CNN journalists were exceptional. "What should I change it to?" I asked Mike.

"Here, give me the remote. You want to watch the news, right?"

"Right."

"Watch this," he said. Mike changed the channel to Fox News.

I had never heard of Fox News before, as that channel wasn't part of our Peruvian cable package. As I watched it now, a Fox News anchor interviewed a woman wearing a tee shirt decorated with the American flag. She was supporting George W. Bush for president. Bush was the governor of

Texas at the time, and he struck me as a charismatic man with a strong Texas accent. I struggled to understand him but noticed that he displayed a happy-go-lucky attitude. "Why are you voting for Governor Bush?" the interviewer asked the woman.

"Because he'll take the country back from the liberals," she responded proudly.

"How so?"

"He'll get rid of the corruption in Washington. Haven't you seen what's happening to our country?"

I certainly hadn't. I couldn't understand why this woman and I had such opposing views on the country's financial and political health. I was intrigued by the notion that so many people truly believed that the United States was in bad shape, even though its economy appeared to be strong and its unemployment rate was at an all-time low.

Also, corruption? In the United States? Corruption was something that happened in South America, not in the United States. In 2000, the president of Peru was Alberto Fujimori, a Peruvian of Japanese descent. He had become the president in 1990 after a hard-fought election against Mario Vargas Llosa, one of Peru's greatest writers, and inherited Alan Garcia's legacy: a country immersed in deep political, social, and financial crises. The country had defaulted on its financial obligations, and its economy was in shambles. Peruvians lived in fear of the Shining Path and MRTA. It was not a great time for my homeland.

However, once Fujimori took office, things started to change. He has been credited with restoring Peru's macroeconomic stability and defeating the Shining Path and MRTA. Many, however, would argue that he gets more credit than he actually deserves. In many ways, all the good he did with his right hand, he erased with his left, when he became a dictator. And as with most dictatorships, corruption and the abuse of power were at the heart of his government. During the last years of his tenure, Fujimori controlled many of the Peruvian media outlets, who claimed that he could do no wrong. His government prosecuted many newspapers or television shows that opposed his administration.

At the time, I didn't think that any form of manipulation or bias occurred in the United States' media. I assumed that only happened in developing countries. It turns out that I was wrong.

We continued watching Fox News, which showed interview after interview with regular citizens expressing their displeasure with the Clinton administration. I was confused and felt like I had entered a new world of information.

"Mike, do you get most of your news from Fox?" I asked.

"Pretty much."

I waited for a few seconds before I tentatively asked, "Can I ask you a few questions about the Republican Party?"

He paused and raised his eyebrows as if I had asked something terrible. "I'll tell you what. Evan should be stopping by in a few minutes. You can ask him," Mike said. Evan was a close friend of the Martins. He lived and worked on an adjacent farm and was a young veteran who had fought in the Gulf War. Mike knew that Evan would be excited to answer my questions.

Soon after, Jenny called Mike, asking him to come help her with her dress. "Santiago, I'll be right back. Evan should get here soon," Mike said.

Evan didn't take long to arrive. He opened the door and walked right into the house. "Mike? Anybody home?" he shouted. He was a large man with a deep voice.

"Mike's upstairs. I assume you're Evan?" I said.

"Hey, yes, I'm Evan. Are you Sebastian?" he asked politely.

"Santiago," I responded.

"Oh, sorry. Potatoes, pot*aa*-toes," he said, smiling.

"No worries. Have a seat." Evan sat down next to me but didn't say much. We watched Fox News until Mike and Jenny came downstairs.

"Evan! Good to see you. Are you ready to go?" Mike asked.

Jenny looked lovely. She used every opportunity she could to dress up. Evan noticed and complimented her: "Looking great, Jenny. Mike, if you're not careful, I'll steal her from you."

"I'd like to see you try," Mike responded. They all laughed.

On our way to the restaurant, I thought about my question to Mike about the Republican Party and wondered whether it had been inappropriate. I wasn't sure if I should bring it up again.

Fortunately, at the restaurant, after we all made some small talk, Mike said, "Evan, this young man has some questions for you."

"Oh yeah? Okay, what are they?" Evan asked.

"I have questions about the Republican Party," I said tentatively.

"Okay. What do you want to know?" I was relieved that he seemed receptive to my question. Perhaps I hadn't committed a major social faux pas after all.

"Are you a Republican?"

"Yes."

"Why?"

"Well, that's easy." He lifted his hand and used his fingers to count off his answers: "I don't want the government interfering with my life. I'm pro-life. I want to keep my right to bear arms. I want my government to be fiscally conservative. I'm a Christian."

That was a complicated answer, but it almost felt rehearsed. Evan's response mirrored many of the comments I'd heard while we watched Fox News.

"What do you think of President Clinton?" I asked.

"He's a liar—the most corrupt politician I know."

This left me speechless. I had watched Fox News for the first time that day and had seen several people giving similar answers. A man wearing a shirt displaying a gun gave a speech about the need to protect his right to bear arms. A lady had talked about protecting babies from abortion. Another man had complained about the expansion of entitlements. All of them had profoundly disliked the Clinton administration and labeled Clinton himself "corrupt."

I asked a few more questions but stopped when I noticed that Mike started to look uncomfortable. Maybe discussing politics over dinner was a bit of a social faux pas in the United States after all.

To change the subject, Mike asked me about the soccer season, and Jenny talked about how much my English had improved. They talked about their farms and the prospects for the year. However, I couldn't stop thinking about what Evan had said. I began to question my own opinions on the matter.

When I got home, I turned on the television and flipped through different news channels. Each channel appeared to have a different take on the same facts. It finally dawned on me that the United States had a bipartisan media. The "can do no wrong" mentality of one side was contrasted by an "it's all your fault" mentality of the other. Negative ads appeared on all channels.

It took me some time to fully process this information. I realized that I needed to be very careful with the information presented to me by the media. I didn't have a personal opinion on whether Fox News or CNN or any other channel was right or wrong. I just knew that I needed to find a balance. How, though? I wasn't sure. The one thing I knew for sure though was that the United States' media was more divided than I had ever imagined.

Chapter Twenty-Two
MR. VICE-PRESIDENT, I AM BLEEDING

May 27, 2000

Over the summer, I went on a trip to the East Coast to visit my aunt and uncle in the Big Apple. They had moved to New York City from Peru in the 1980s and built a life in the United States. I didn't go to New York by myself, though. My host family had planned a trip to that state to visit Clark, my other host brother, and to see Vice-President Al Gore speak at the West Point graduation ceremony. (This last part was considered a bit of a joke though, since my host parents were Republicans.)

So how did this Peruvian teenager get to attend this prestigious school's graduation ceremony? Well, Clark was graduating from West Point, so my host family made the trip to be present at his graduation. It was a proud weekend for my host parents and a unique experience for me. Since I enjoyed reading about history, I thought this would be a great opportunity to learn, first hand, some American history. And Edward was the perfect host for that.

Before the graduation ceremony, Edward, Carrie, and I walked around the West Point campus. Based on the way Edward talked about it, it seemed like he knew everything about the place. I learned, among other things, about the

Revolutionary War and the fact that George Washington considered West Point to be the most important military location in the country.

In addition to learning about American history, walking around West Point also made me realize that this country is blessed from a landscaping perspective. I didn't see many water sprinklers, but all the green areas were just that: green. In many instances, whenever we stopped to learn more about a historic location, I observed and appreciated the beautifully manicured lawns, something I didn't take for granted.

I like to believe that I have a green thumb, as I have taken care of a few plants in my life. In fact, for a few years, I grew a bonsai tree in my home in Peru. Bonsai is the Japanese art form of growing miniature trees in small containers and carefully shaping the tree and its roots. It's a beautiful art form and a great way to grow small trees indoors. It was somewhat difficult to maintain my bonsai tree in my hometown though, since, unlike Lima, Arequipa is a dry city. Plants need to be watered constantly there; otherwise, they'll struggle to grow or even just simply die. My bonsai tree enjoyed a couple years of healthy growth, but it ended up dying. Not because of the dry Arequipa weather, though. My bonsai tree's cause of death was determined to be "unintentional drowning."

I had read several books on bonsai care, and my little tree did well until I left it in the care of our maid, Jacinta, for a few weeks one summer when I went to Trujillo, a city in the northern part of Peru, for a track and field national tournament. Since some of my relatives lived there, my family decided to stay with them for a couple weeks after the competition. During that time, Jacinta was tasked with watering the plant every other day. I had purchased a small spray bottle and learned that my tree needed three pumps of water every other day. No more than that, though, as bonsais are sensitive to overwatering.

Although I had given Jacinta specific instructions, she didn't follow them. When I returned to Arequipa, Jacinta opened the door with a puzzled face. She told me that she had watered the tree every other day, just as I had told her, for the first few days, but then she noticed that the tree seemed a bit "dry." She gave it more water and couldn't understand why its leaves began to fall. She thought it was because it needed even more water. After a few days, my tree was no longer a beautifully manicured plant. It had lost all its leaves and become a tiny piece of wood.

Most plants in my hometown didn't die from overwatering, but rather due to the rough climate conditions. Arequipa's high altitude and dry climate make it difficult for plants to thrive there. Unless one has an irrigation system— and most homes don't—patches of green are scarce. In other words, except for the summer months, when Arequipa suffers from floods due to the seasonal rainfall, the grass is only green if you water it.

Conversely, in some parts of the United States, it seemed as though the spring magically made everything bloom. In Iowa, as soon as the snow began to melt, brown pastures turned green. The change didn't take long, either. All of a sudden, tree branches went from being brown sticks to green, leafy oxygen producers. I marveled at this phenomenon.

*   *   *

"Santiago, it's time to go," Edward said. We had been exploring the campus for a couple of hours. Although we had tickets with assigned seats, thousands of people were attending the graduation ceremony, and he wanted to avoid any lines that may inevitably form to enter the stadium.

As we walked toward the stadium, I noticed a great deal of security. I also saw some very serious-looking people walking around with earpieces. I asked James who they were, and he responded, "Secret service agents. They're here because of the vice-president."

I had seen these tall, intimidating, and somewhat serious people in movies, but I had never expected to see them in real life. This was a big deal for me. Growing up, I had great admiration for the United States, and it had been a dream of mine to see its high-ranking officials. However, I didn't know much about Vice-President Al Gore. I only knew that people said he would become the president if President Clinton were removed from office.

Once we got to our seats, I didn't say much. I observed. This wasn't an ordinary graduation. Parents, many of them members or former members of one of the branches of the military, were clearly bursting with pride. The cadets wore uniforms of a gray, long-sleeved wool jacket, white pants, and a white hat. The civilians' clothing ranged from khakis and polos to full suits for the men and mostly dresses for the women. I wore cargo shorts, a tee shirt, and my black University of Iowa hat. I later learned that the event dress code called for nicer attire, but I didn't get the memo at the time.

After the cadets found their seats on the field, a couple of people on the stage said a few words and a song started playing. It was "The Star-Spangled Banner," the United States' national anthem.

"Santiago, your hat," James said, pointing at my hat. I hurriedly took it off like the other men around me and respectfully crossed my hands in front of me. I wasn't a United States citizen, so I didn't put my hand on my chest, as most people did.

While watching Americans sing their national anthem before a sporting event was impressive, watching thousands of military families sing it at what was ostensibly a military event was moving. As I looked out at the crowd, I noticed how some parents were overcome with pride. After the national anthem, I took a deep breath. "That was intense," I told Carrie, who was in tears. She smiled. She was overwhelmed as well.

Eventually, Vice-President Gore came onstage. He was far away, but I could tell it was definitely him up there. He congratulated the graduating cadets and their parents. Frankly, I couldn't understand much of what he said. The combination of not being a native speaker and being stuck next to a lady who couldn't stop talking to her husband ruined the moment for me. When the vice-president was done speaking, everyone applauded.

The temperature kept rising throughout the ceremony, and I began to wonder how long the cadets would have to sit under the hot sun. Although I was wearing shorts and sitting in the shade, I was starting to sweat, and the poor cadets had to wear heavy, long-sleeve wool jackets. I'm sure they were growing uncomfortable, and I hoped the graduation ceremony would end soon, for their sakes.

Fortunately, just a few minutes later, all the cadets stood. An official on the stage administered the Oath of Allegiance, the cadets sang the "Army Song," and a speaker gave the cadets one final order: "Class of 2000, dismissed!" At that, the cadets grabbed their hats and tossed them up in the air, breaking the silence with a loud cheer. The crowd applauded, and the stadium was filled with expressions of joy. Parents and other relatives in the stands congratulated each other.

After that, we made our way down to the field to congratulate Clark. He was clutching his head as he looked around for his hat.

"Oh my gosh, Clark! What happened? Are you okay?" Carrie asked, worried.

"Yes, I'm fine, Mom," he said. "Stupid hat," he added under his breath. Apparently, during the hat toss, one of the hats had fallen on his head at a dangerous angle and cut him, causing him to start bleeding. It wasn't too bad, but it was definitely unexpected.

All the Novaks and I gathered around Clark to congratulate him. Despite the blood on his head, he wore a wide smile. After a few minutes, Clark had to hurry away to take care of some paperwork associated with his graduation and commissioning. My host family wanted to stay on campus for a bit longer and go to the bookstore to purchase some souvenirs.

It had been a long, hot day for me, and I was ready to go back to the hotel to rest. "Santiago, dismissed!" I whispered. Unfortunately, the order didn't work for me.

Chapter Twenty-Three
MEETING MY RELATIVES

May 29, 2000

The plan was to spend a couple of days with my host brother at West Point before heading to New York City with my Peruvian relatives. Those two days were a unique experience for me, as I didn't grow up in a military family. In fact, I grew up with a deep distrust of the Peruvian military. After all, I grew up in a country where allegations of corruption in the military were on the news every day. I respected the American armed forces, though. They were always portrayed as the highest standard for any military in the world. As a result, I spent most of my time at West Point observing, asking questions, and trying to learn from the experience.

After two days surrounded by American military personnel, though, it was definitely time to take a break from my American life with an Iowan farm family, going to a Midwestern high school, and listening to and speaking English all the time. I was ready to meet my uncle and aunt, make the drive to New York City, and spend a few weeks with them.

Alberto is my father's brother, and he met his wife, Emilia, when they were children. They grew up in the same neighborhood. Although Emilia immigrated to the United

States in her early twenties, they kept in touch. Years later, they married, and Alberto moved to New York with her.

Since Alberto had left Peru when I was a small child, I mostly knew about him and his wife through stories my parents told. Alberto had been a popular soccer player in my hometown's local league.

When they arrived at West Point, Alberto and Emilia stopped by our hotel. I gave each a hug. I could tell that they were just as excited to see me as I was to see them. It was great to finally meet these relatives I had only ever known through pictures and long-distance phone calls. Alberto talked with Carrie and Edward for a few minutes before shaking their hands and exchanging hugs. With that, I said goodbye to my host family and jumped into Alberto's car. In a few minutes, we were on our way to *"La Gran Manzana,"* New York City.

After a few minutes of small talk—all in Spanish, which was a delightful treat—my aunt asked, "So how's your trip going? How's Iowa?"

Although they had lived in the United States for many years, they had never visited the Midwest. For them, Iowa was almost as foreign as it was for me when I first arrived in Mount Vernon. They knew that Iowa was flat, full of corn, and rather cold and snowy during winter, but that was the extent of their knowledge.

I started by telling them that Iowa wasn't what I had expected. I didn't really know what I had expected, but if I had any expectations, Iowa wasn't it. I told them about the language barrier and about how wonderful my host family had been. I shared how impressive it was that a small-town public high school had more technology than my private city high school in Peru. I told them about prom, my American friends, and my soccer season. In short, I said that I was having the time of my life.

"You're not still in your honeymoon period, are you?" my aunt asked after this long monologue.

"What do you mean?"

"It's that time when everything is still new and shiny. Everything is exciting, and you learn new things every day," she said. She explained that, generally, there were usually four different stages for newcomers. First, there's a honeymoon period. Depending on the person and the length of their trip, that stage's length could vary.

Next, there's a period when most people become frustrated with their surroundings. This is especially true for people living in a country where everyone around them speaks a different language from their own. During this period, even small things can trigger anxiety. This is the stage when many begin to miss their home country and experience feelings of loneliness and even depression. At this point, going back home doesn't sound like a bad idea.

With time, most people enter a new phase. Their surroundings become more familiar, it's easier to make new friends, and most begin to understand the local language. Certain details that seemed confusing at first start to make sense and become part of the person's life. At this point, the adjustment to the new environment is almost complete.

Finally, most people, though not all, enter a period where they accept their surroundings for what they are. The period of "comparing and contrasting" is generally over, and most begin to accept that certain things are just different from what they're like at home and that there's no point in trying to change it all.

"So, Santiago, in which period are you?" Alberto asked.

"I think I'm beginning to adjust," I answered.

"Why do you say that?"

"I mean, I continue to experience new things, but the period of frustration seems to be over for the most part. I think."

"Well, it's not an exact science," Emilia said. "Keep that in mind. But it's good for you to be aware of these phases."

"How do you know about them?" I asked. "I mean, you weren't an exchange student."

"We weren't exchange students, but we both moved to a different country," Emilia pointed out.

"I'd bet that most people who change their environment go through a similar process," Alberto added.

"What do you mean?"

"We've seen it everywhere. We have friends who went through the same process in college or even when changing jobs," Alberto said.

"When we first came to the United States, things weren't easy. At the beginning, everything was new for both of us, too. We became frustrated with many things. We compared our lives in New York to our lives in Arequipa all the time," Emilia said.

"For a long time, we weren't happy in New York. Most people back in Peru don't know this, but things were difficult for us," Alberto said.

"You never said anything about it, though. Why?" I asked.

"Why would we? We had no reason to make people worry about us," Emilia said.

"If you didn't like it, then why did you stay?"

"That's a loaded question, Santiago, but we can say that, with time, we adapted," Alberto said, noticing that the conversation was getting a bit dense. He then changed the subject: "Are you hungry? Do you want to have some *ceviche*?"

"Yes!" I responded. It had been six months since I'd had Peruvian food, and I was craving it. "Where are we going?"

"Patterson. It's in New Jersey," Emilia responded. I later learned that Patterson has a large Peruvian population.

When we arrived in Patterson, we entered a Peruvian restaurant. It looked like a house that had been remodeled into a business. There were six or seven tables covered with tablecloths. Each table had small bowls of *canchita*, which is a kind of Peruvian popcorn. While Mexican restaurants have free chips and salsa as an appetizer, Peruvian restaurants have *canchita*. Peruvian music played in the background. Paintings of Peruvian landscapes and posters with popular Peruvian soccer players decorated the room. Alberto and I ordered *ceviche*, while Emilia ordered *arroz con mariscos*, a dish prepared with fried rice and seafood.

Although the restaurant had a humble appearance, the food didn't disappoint. The exciting part, however, was just getting to see Alberto and Emilia. Meeting my relatives in a foreign country was special.

After our meal, we drove to Brooklyn, where Alberto and Emilia lived. I asked whether we would get to visit Times Square that day, and Alberto said that we wouldn't. They were both tired, and to visit Times Square properly, they wanted to take me on a walking tour of the city. That wasn't going to happen on my first day.

Once in Brooklyn, we stopped outside of their place, which was a small condo in an Italian neighborhood. Alberto helped me carry my bags inside. After Emilia offered me a glass of water, she showed me to the guest room, and I took my bags there.

"Santiago, want to help me park the car?" Alberto asked after I dropped my bags in my room.

"Sure," I said. I thought it was an odd question until I realized why he'd asked me to go with him. It took us about twenty minutes to find a place to park. When we finally found one, the space was so small that I didn't think it was big enough for his car.

"There's no way you can fit the car in that spot, Alberto," I said. He rolled his eyes and asked me to get out and let him know if he got too close to the vehicles parked in front of and behind his car. He put the car in reverse and started to park.

"A little more... a little more... stop!" I shouted. After I told him to stop, he jumped out of his car to check how close he was to the other vehicles.

"What are you doing?" he asked. "I have plenty of space."

He got back in his car and kept going in reverse and then moving forward until he started to gently bump the other cars. I didn't say anything else. Instead, I watched him "make" space for his car. A couple of minutes later, he got out of his vehicle. "Ready?" he asked and turned to head back to the condo.

"You just hit those cars! Aren't you worried they'll say something?"

"Who? The cars?" he said, laughing.

"No, the owners," I said as I rolled my eyes.

"Bumpers are for bumping. It's just a love tap," he assured me. I had never thought about bumpers that way before.

On our walk back to their condo, I noticed that several cars were parked so close that one could barely walk between them. And it wasn't just the vehicles that were parked close to each other; most homes appeared to share a wall, just like homes did in Peru. Even though I was still in the United States, this world was definitely different than the world I had experienced in Iowa.

Chapter Twenty-Four
THE BIG APPLE

June 7, 2000

Many people who visit New York City only visit Manhattan. Central Park, Times Square, and Wall Street are at the top of most tourists' must-see lists. Not many have the chance to experience the other boroughs. Luckily, I did.

Since Alberto and Emilia lived in Brooklyn, I spent considerable time exploring that borough. They had lived in Queens—which has a large Latin American population—in the past, so they also made sure that I visited some of its iconic places, too. Then I asked Alberto if we could visit the Bronx, and he had no issues taking me to that borough and sharing a bit of its history. They also took me to Staten Island, the most suburban of the boroughs. Although I could write several pages on each borough, my first day visiting Manhattan was the most memorable part of my trip.

Alberto and Emilia took the day off work for our "walking tour" of Manhattan. Alberto worked for a small electronics store installing home air-conditioning systems, Emilia worked in accounts payable at a small manufacturing company, and neither of them had trouble getting the day off. They planned it out in great detail and were excited to introduce me to the city's most well-known locations. If you ever decide to do a similar walking tour, your senses will appreciate the experience, though your feet will likely need to be immersed in an ice bucket afterwards.

We set out early, and Alberto drove us to a bus station in Brooklyn. From there, we took a bus to Staten Island and the Staten Island Ferry. For those who have never visited New York, the Staten Island Ferry is one of the last remaining vestiges of the New York City ferry system. Once on the ferry, the ride to lower Manhattan took about twenty-five minutes. From the ferry, we had a perfect view of the Statute of Liberty, Ellis Island, and lower Manhattan.

Alberto and Emilia suggested that I don't take too many pictures. They encouraged me to "live" the experience instead. "There will be plenty of time for pictures," Alberto assured me. Although this proved to be difficult, I tried to follow their advice as much as possible.

As we got closer to lower Manhattan, I observed the city's massive skyscrapers and thought that it all felt like a dream. This was my first encounter with New York's skyscrapers, and I couldn't believe that I was actually approaching the famed "Big Apple." More than anything though, I thought about my maternal grandfather's New York City dreams.

My mother's father had been a banker. His bank was connected to a popular New York-based bank, and he frequently mentioned this fact to me when I was a child. One of his dreams was to some day travel to the United States, visit the New York bank's main office in Manhattan, and walk around Central Park, Broadway, and Wall Street. Unfortunately, a heart attack took his life far too soon and before he could take that trip. Now, as I observed the skyscrapers of Manhattan, I smiled. I was sure that my visit to

New York City would have made him happy. For a moment, I felt like I was living his dream for him and that a part of him had finally made it to New York.

When we arrived in lower Manhattan, we walked to a street corner to get a hot dog. Alberto said that I should not get used to eating hot dogs because they are unhealthy, but that I had to try one in New York City.

From there, we walked to the Charging Bull, a bronze sculpture that stood in the Financial District. Alberto explained that it represented capitalism and that it was the symbol of financial optimism and prosperity, unlike the bear, which represented pessimism. I wasn't sure why the city's forefathers had picked a bull and a bear to represent those feelings. I assumed it was a uniquely American thing, just like picking a donkey and an elephant to represent their prominent political parties. I would have picked something different than a bull. Maybe something a little happier, like a dog.

The interesting thing about the Charging Bull is that many tourists don't take pictures of its front. Instead, many walk around to the back of the bull and take pictures of its rather prominent testicles. *When in Rome*, I thought as I took a picture with the bull's balls.

Next, we went up the island to the World Trade Center. At the time, the Twin Towers were still part of New York's iconic skyline, and I stared at them for some time. The sheer size of each column was intimidating. I noticed that my neck muscles were getting stiff and realized that my neck would probably hurt at the end of the day. Being in New York for the first time, I was bound to look up a lot.

Alberto must have noticed me rubbing my neck, as he asked, "Santiago, ready for a change?"

"Sure, what's next?"

"Chinatown," Alberto said with a smile.

Chinatown was a neighborhood in lower Manhattan, home to the highest concentration of Chinese people in New York. At least, that's what Alberto told me. Entering this district was a complete culture shock. Within two blocks, I felt like I was in a different country. Although it reminded me of walking around Lima's Chinatown, this was different, as New York City's was much bigger and more complex.

Alberto pulled me into a small store and said a few words to the owner in English. Emilia seemed a little nervous, and I asked her why we were stopping there. "Your uncle wants to buy you a watch," she said.

A rather small man with Asian features opened a door to a back room. We entered, and he quickly closed the door behind us. The room contained thousands of watches.

"Pick one," Alberto said.

"No, don't worry about it. I don't need a watch," I responded.

"Just pick one, Santiago," Emilia said. She seemed to be in a hurry now.

I looked at a few watches and noticed that Emilia had started to pace the small room. I grabbed a couple of watches and tried them on. Even though there were thousands of them, nothing grabbed my attention.

We were in this room for about ten minutes when Emilia walked toward the door. "Let's go, Alberto," Emilia said, opening the door. Alberto followed her, and so did I. I had no idea what had just happened.

We walked out of the store, and no one said a word. Out on the street, Alberto and Emilia started bickering over our short visit to the watch store. When they noticed me trying to listen in on their conversation, Emilia turned to me and said, "I don't like going to those stores, and he knows it."

"Why?"

"She thinks they're dangerous," Alberto responded.

When Emilia first moved to the United States, she had worked in a factory close to Chinatown. She had become acquainted with some people who lived there, and they told her stories about the area and how it could be dangerous at times. Alberto explained that the goods in the store we visited were probably contraband, and this made Emilia anxious.

That surprised me—not because Emilia was nervous, but because I didn't think the United States had an issue with importing goods illegally. It turned out that I was terribly wrong. Importing illegal goods was a big problem in major port cities like New York and Miami.

In the southern part of Peru, buying contraband was the normal way of doing business in some border towns. Although laws prohibited the distribution and marketing of contraband, there were many places where one could buy such goods at a fraction of the price one would pay at a regular store. In fact, many Peruvians would travel for hours to find those cheaper goods, without caring how the goods entered the country.

"Emi, I just wanted to see if Santiago liked a watch. We don't ever come over here, so I thought we would try to find something," Alberto said to Emilia as he put his arm around her to give her a hug.

"Yeah, yeah, sure," Emilia said, a smile returning to her face. "As long as you don't actually buy anything there, I'm good."

"Fine. Let's keep walking."

Next, we walked by the Empire State building, an American architectural marvel. It made me think about Tom Hanks meeting Meg Ryan there in *Sleepless in Seattle*, a charming romantic comedy from the early 1990s. I pictured the scene in which a giant heart appeared on all four sides of the building. *That* was the United States I had always imagined: the one depicted in movies and television shows. I felt like I was finally experiencing the "real" United States. We didn't go into the Empire State Building, but the mere fact of walking by it made my heart race.

"It's time for lunch," Alberto announced. "Do you want to have a slice of New York pizza?"

"Sure. After all, pizza is pizza," I said.

That was the wrong thing to say. He looked at me as if I had committed a grave sin. New Yorkers are proud of their pizza, and he made sure I learned that fact.

We walked by Madison Square Garden and stopped at a hole-in-the-wall place to have this venerated variety of pizza. Perhaps it's because I was hungry, but that thin-crusted pizza was as delicious as the most exquisite dish one could order at a high-end Italian restaurant.

Emilia, as usual, wasn't impressed. She had very particular taste buds and had developed a habit of quickly criticizing food. Plus, she was getting tired.

The next part of our adventure was, to me, the most marvelous of it all. We walked up the streets filled with yellow taxis, luxurious vehicles, both homeless people and rich people, all sorts of lights, and a rather distinctive smell—the smell of a city that never sleeps. As we approached the most iconic display of capitalism in the Western Hemisphere, a broad smile appeared on my face. All those words my grandfather had once said to me, all the stories he had told, and all his dreams were becoming a reality for me. Once again, I felt that he was experiencing a world that he had admired but could never visit, through me.

"Are you okay?" Alberto asked. He must have noticed that I was overwhelmed with emotion.

"Yes. Never been better," I responded, giving him a pat on the back.

The lights continued to intensify, more and more billboards appeared all around us, and the streets became fuller and fuller. I heard someone shout something in English, two people carrying on a conversation in Spanish, a couple discussing their next destination in German, and a few teenagers holding oddly shaped cameras and speaking in what I assumed was Mandarin. Every skin tone and several different languages were represented in New York City. Short people, tall people, the super fit, the overweight, rich, poor, old, young—you name it, you could find it in that place. The diversity was astonishing. So were the lights.

"Welcome to Times Square," Emilia said.

Although there were plenty of tourists roaming around Times Square, I don't think that any of them were as thunderstruck as I was. My senses were overstimulated by every part of this place. My eyes attempted to absorb each and every billboard and were attracted by their lights, each of which was brighter than the last. Every turn I took, a different smell appeared in my nostrils. My ears revolted at a police siren, children screaming, teenagers rapping furiously on the street, and the music coming out of each commercial establishment. I touched different types of fabric in a store as I curiously immersed my hands in a pile of "I Heart NY" tee shirts. Even my taste buds were stimulated when my uncle bought me some bright pink cotton candy from a street vendor. Although I knew I couldn't afford much here, I felt like I was in heaven.

We spent about two hours in Times Square, and they were the first of many that I would spend in that part of town in the following days.

"Are we still going to Central Park?" Emilia asked Alberto at one point. They were both exhausted, especially Emilia, who wasn't used to walking that much.

"Santiago, what do you think? Want to walk up the street for a few blocks?" Alberto asked.

"Yes, but only if Emilia can make it," I said. Although I wanted to be considerate, and my feet were in desperate need of an ice bath, I was still eager to continue exploring Manhattan.

Emilia turned and looked at me with a stunned expression. She exclaimed, "I can make it. I'll prove it to you."

Once we made it to the park, we stopped at a local coffee shop to grab a drink and something to eat before crossing the street. It was seven p.m., and we were dangerously hungry. We grabbed some tea and small sandwiches to get us through the rest of the day.

"Alberto, when was the last time we took someone on this walking tour?" Emilia said.

"About five years ago, when my sister came to visit," Alberto responded.

"That's right. Let's never do it again," Emilia said, laughing.

Our walk through Central Park was relatively short. Emilia and Alberto were not in the mood to walk anymore, so I wasn't surprised when they agreed with my suggestion that we head home for the day. I was tired, too, and although I could have kept walking for a few more hours, I understood it was time to go.

We didn't take the ferry back to Staten Island. Instead, we took the subway. I had never ridden on a subway before, and prior to my trip to New York, many people had told me that New York's subway was filthy and full of strange, dangerous people. However, I thought it was a delightful experience. Perhaps I was simply so startled by the idea of being onboard an electric train that I overlooked the dirt and unpleasant smells. In any event, I enjoyed the ride and thought of it as another unique experience.

We made it to Brooklyn in a few minutes and walked to Alberto's car at the station. After a short car ride, we were back home. Emilia immediately turned on the TV and sat down on the couch with a bowl of *canchita* to watch another episode of her favorite *telenovela*. Alberto went to his room to lie down. I took a shower and got ready for bed. As I jumped into my bed, I reminisced about this amazing, magical day. *What a beautiful day*, I thought.

Chapter Twenty-Five
LOST IN NEW YORK

June 22, 2000

In the following weeks, Alberto and Emilia took me to the most iconic spots in New York City. We visited the Twin Towers and the Empire State building again. I still have a picture of myself standing in front of the World Trade Center, when the towers still defined the New York skyline. We visited the American Museum of Natural History, the Museum of Modern Art, and the Guggenheim Museum. They drove me to Queens, to Harlem, and even to New Jersey. Although both of them had jobs, they tried to show me as much as they could. "This is the time of your life when you need to be exposed to new things. You need to open your mind to new experiences," Emilia said to me every so often.

However, despite all her talk about "opening my mind," Emilia didn't let me move around the city by myself. Even though I had turned eighteen that month, Emilia and Alberto made it clear that I was still their responsibility. Like most teenagers, I thought I could do anything on my own, and I assumed they were overreacting. I didn't understand why they were so vehement about this until we got separated during one of our Manhattan adventures.

One day, Emilia and I went to Manhattan to meet Alberto, who worked in the city. Emilia had taken the afternoon off to run some errands and thought it would be fun to walk around Times Square and visit some stores after she was done with her errands. I particularly wanted to go to the Virgin store, listen to some music, and perhaps buy a CD. Emilia wanted to check out the newest toys at the Disney store. She had a strange fascination with Mickey Mouse.

We arrived in Manhattan around five p.m., and Alberto would meet us in a couple of hours. Although I had heard our meeting location, I hadn't paid much attention, as I relied on Emilia to get us there. Once in Times Square, I figured we would spend thirty or forty minutes in the Disney store and then head to the Virgin store for the remainder of the time.

We walked into the Disney store, and the place was a nightmare. Dozens of kids were screaming at their parents so they would feel forced to buy them the latest toy or stuffed animal. I liked Disney, but the thought of spending more than ten minutes in that place made me cringe. "Emilia, I'll wait for you at the door. Is that okay?" I asked.

"Fine, but I might be here for a while."

"No worries. Just don't leave without me," I joked.

"Okay, I'll meet you at the door at 5:30 p.m.," she said.

"You got it."

I walked to the door and stood outside to people-watch. New York City is one of the best cities in the United States to observe other people. I was overwhelmed to think that behind every person, there was a different story and that New York City had millions of them. I wandered up and down the block, daydreaming. Unfortunately, when I daydream, I usually lose track of time, and this time wasn't any different. When I looked at my watch, it was almost six p.m.

I ran back to the Disney store to look for Emilia, but I couldn't find her. How could I? There were hundreds, if not thousands, of people walking in all directions. I panicked. I didn't have a cell phone. Heck, I didn't even know their numbers or their address. I was lost in the middle of Times Square.

In retrospect, I should have waited for Emilia and Alberto at the door of the Disney store. Instead, in my panicked state, I began to walk around the block, hoping that I would miraculously find them. I thought about taking a taxi, but what would I tell the driver? "Sir, take me to Alberto and Emilia's home in Brooklyn?" That wasn't going to work.

After walking aimlessly for a few minutes, I realized that I needed a plan to get home. Since I couldn't remember where Alberto said he would meet us and I couldn't find Emilia, I would just have to find a way to get back to Brooklyn on my own.

I had taken the bus and the subway with them before, but I usually just tagged along without paying attention to where I was going. I got on the bus they chose and took the train they wanted to take. All I could remember was that we had taken Line B at some point. At least it was a starting point. I walked to a subway station and got a Metro Card. Then I found a subway map and tried to decipher where I needed to go. I knew they lived in Brooklyn, so I looked for all the lines that went to that borough. There it was: Line B, which went right into the heart of Brooklyn. Of course, so did Lines D, N, Q, and F.

What now? Eeny, meeny, miny, moe? I didn't think so. I had to go with my gut, take Line B, and hope for the best.

I jumped on the subway and prayed that I was right. If I weren't, where would I go? I had spent all my cash on the Metro Card, and the only phone number I knew was my mother's in Peru. I thought about approaching a police officer to ask for help, but I wasn't that desperate yet.

The subway was, of course, underground, so I had to try to remember the station names. I knew I needed to exit at the right station, otherwise I would be lost in Brooklyn. I studied the map inside the train and decided to hop off at the exit that seemed the most familiar. Luckily, when I exited that station, my surroundings were indeed familiar. I recognized the Century 21 department store on the corner, the McDonald's across the street, and the Starbucks a block away.

I walked to the bus stop on the corner and looked at the map there. The only thing I could remember was that I needed to get to Seventy-Fourth Street. I found the bus that would take me there and waited for it.

Once on the bus, I sat by the window, observing the environment while trying to remember the route. It all looked familiar, but since it was such a large city, there were too many similar corners and streets.

Finally, we arrived at Seventy-Fourth Street, and I hopped off the bus. It was dark outside by now, and the neighborhood wasn't well-lit. Many of the townhomes looked similar, and it was all confusing. I tried to retrace my steps from earlier in the day. Although it took me about thirty minutes to find their condo, I was eventually successful.

I walked up the stairs to their condo and knocked on the door. Emilia opened it. "Santiago! Where were you? Where did you go?" she exclaimed. She was clearly upset. I had never seen her angry before, so I thought a joke would lighten the mood.

"You left me," I said, smiling.

She stared at me for a long moment and then turned and walked into the living room. I didn't know how to interpret her behavior, so I followed her, not saying anything. I was tired and thirsty, so I walked into the kitchen to grab a glass of Inca Kola, a Peruvian soft drink. With a full glass in my hand, I approached Emilia again.

"How was your night?" I asked, still smiling.

"How?" she repeated, her voice still angry. She grabbed the newspaper, folded it up, and hit me on the head with it. "That's how." With that, she finally smiled back at me.

Emilia had called Alberto at work when she couldn't find me. He had left work before his shift was over, and they had searched for me for quite a while. Obviously, they couldn't find me, so they drove back home, hoping that I had already made it back safely. They thought I had their address in my wallet and trusted that I would somehow make it home. Emilia said that they were getting ready to call the police just before I arrived at the house.

Just as Emilia was finishing telling me off, Alberto came out of his room. I jokingly told him that Emilia had left me. He laughed, though Emilia didn't. Although I had made it back home without a scratch, he had a talk with me later that night. He explained that I was their responsibility and that I needed to be more careful. I apologized to both of them.

Years later, Emilia and I still talk about that day and argue about how things transpired. She recalls it as "The Night Santiago Got Lost in Manhattan." I refer to it as "The Night Emilia, in an Irresponsible Manner, Left Me in Manhattan by Myself." Of course, I know it was all my fault.

Chapter Twenty-Six
MENTORS

June 27, 2000

When friends ask me about my first year in the United States, I usually tell them about my adventures in Mount Vernon, the unforgettable experience at Times Square, and my love/hate relationship with the Midwest's ever-changing weather. I generally don't share my most personal thoughts and feelings, and I tend not to talk about some people who made a deep impression on me.

I've been told that it is people, not money, that can change lives. Even though I agree with that statement for the most part, I would say that money can change lives, too. I understand that if a person doesn't have enough money to eat, having more of it can make a big impact. Throughout my life, I've heard many argue that you need money to live well and that people with money tend to live longer and healthier lives because they have access to better food and healthcare. I can attest that being able to put healthy food on the table, living under a decent roof in a good neighborhood, and having access to adequate healthcare has improved my standard of living. Having money can, and usually does, make a significant difference in a person's life.

To me, however, money hasn't been the ultimate goal of my life, nor has it been the starting point for it. So what has it been? Well, aside from God, the answer for me has been people.

People have the ability to make you or break you. People can raise you up or try to bring you down. People can comfort you or make you feel worthless. People, not money, are at the beginning and the end of one's life.

When I was fourteen years old, I visited my paternal grandfather for the last time. He had been battling cancer for several years, and his body couldn't fight the illness anymore. A couple of days before he passed away, I went to his room to say my last goodbye. He had always been a man of very few words. In fact, I think we had our longest conversation ever on that occasion. We talked about my schoolwork and about the track season. It was mostly small talk. Then, when he realized that we didn't have much more to talk about, he held my hand and looked at me. "You know, at the end of your life, all you can take with you is your memories. So make sure you make good ones," he said. Those were his last words to me.

He couldn't take any material possessions with him. Although he didn't have much, he had to leave it all behind. On that day, and on his last days with us, money and material possessions didn't bring him comfort. People did. His family and friends did.

This is where Alberto and Emilia made a difference in my life. Although they bought me clothes, fed me, and took me places I had never imagined I would visit, they didn't do this because they had to. They did it because they wanted to. They wanted the best for me even though they barely knew me.

They shared their stories and experiences so I wouldn't make the same mistakes they had. They, and especially Emilia, nagged me so I would learn from their mistakes. Alberto and Emilia guided me in a foreign land and gave me comfort. They were blunt with me when they needed to be and understanding when they saw that I needed it. They were more than just family to me. They behaved like mentors.

I've had many mentors in Peru and in the United States: my parents, my godfather, my brother, other relatives, my host families, and my friends. Some of them have given me career advice. Some have given me financial advice. All of them have given me life advice.

It took me some time to realize that I could find mentors everywhere and from all realms of life. It has taken me even longer to understand that when someone lends me a hand, I should not be afraid or ashamed to take it. In fact, I have learned to lean on the people who are good to me and to protect our relationships. I have learned to be a mentor, too.

Alberto and Emilia raised me up, gave me comfort, and made me a better person. They, with all of their quirks, were my first mentors in the United States. And for that, I will forever be grateful to them.

Chapter Twenty-Seven
COWS, CARS, AND AUTOMATIC TRANSMISSIONS

July 7, 2000

After a few weeks in New York City, Alberto drove me to Newark International Airport to catch my flight back to Cedar Rapids. I wasn't ready to leave them, but I had to continue my exchange program.

Edward picked me up from the airport. It was mid-afternoon, and he was driving James' convertible with the top down. By now, the landscape had changed dramatically. A hot and steamy summer had taken over Iowa. The wind no longer hurt my face, but I could feel my pores opening up, as if I had just stepped into a sauna.

When we arrived in Mount Vernon, we stopped at a red light, and I started to sweat. "It's hot," I said, stating the obvious.

"Just wait until next week, Santiago. We're having a heat wave," he responded, laughing.

It had taken me a while to understand why most Iowans talked and joked about the weather so much in conversations. When it was bitterly cold, many Iowans would observe that it was terrible outside as though they were proud of that fact and then laugh. Meanwhile, I would be worrying about the roads and getting home safely. In the summer, when it was remarkably warm, people would talk about the humidity and the heat with a similar mixture of pride and amusement. I was more concerned about staying hydrated and wearing a proper amount of sunscreen.

We shared the same fundamental concerns, but they looked at the Midwest's extremes in weather with a hint of humor that I lacked for some time. Comedy was generally an outlet for their frustrations, not a literal evaluation of their circumstances.

It may seem trivial, but before moving to another country, no one tells you that each country and each culture has its own unique sense of humor. Only time can teach you to understand and appreciate another culture's humor. Apparently, I still didn't grasp Midwestern humor when it came to the weather.

*   *   *

As soon as we walked into the house, Edward asked me to help him out on the farm that day. We needed to move cattle from one side of the farm to the other.

"Lucky me," I mumbled as I went to my room to drop my bags and get a hat. In just a few hours, I had gone from wandering around among skyscrapers to moving cows across a road.

"Santiago, hurry up," Edward shouted as if one of the cows were having a heart attack.

He apparently couldn't wait for me and headed out to start moving the cows by himself—an impossible task. You needed at least two people, preferably three, to move those four-legged creatures across the road.

Now, you may be wondering why I keep saying "across the road." The Novaks owned land on both sides of the gravel road. They had a barn on one side and the house and, well, another barn on the other side. Every so often, they moved cattle from one side of the road to the other. I initially thought it was so the cows could get a little exercise, but it was apparently because they needed to eat "fresh grass." Plus, one side of the road had a pond in which the cows could swim during the hot summer months.

When I left the house, I ran as fast as I could to help Edward with the difficult task. "Here, Santiago. Grab the stick, open the gate, and make sure the cows don't escape," he instructed.

"What's the stick for?"

"Just give them a nudge if they get rowdy."

There wasn't much time to think about what I had just heard, so I opened the gate and grabbed the stick. Edward started to yell at the cows as I guided them through the gate and onto the road. The good thing about cows is that they tend to move in masses, following a leader. The bad thing about them is that there is always one crazy one in the bunch: the outlier, the free spirit, the reason why it's best to have three people instead of two for such tasks. I'll call the Novaks' rebellious cow "Lucy."

Edward pushed the cows out onto the road, and I acted as a human barrier on the east side of the road. Edward had to act as the human barrier on the west side, but it was physically impossible to push the cows in one direction while also preventing them from wandering.

Lucy was one of the last cows to cross the road, and not being much of a rule-follower, she escaped. Edward tried to grab her, but he stumbled and fell. The gravel wasn't kind to his knees. "Santiago, go get her!" Edward shouted.

I wasted no time and sprinted after Lucy. She wasn't slow for a cow, but she was a cow, nonetheless. I caught up with her and used my stick to try to scare her into turning around. Lucy wasn't afraid of me though, and she kept walking. Luckily, a neighbor who was moving some logs with his tractor recognized my predicament, so he slowly drove his tractor toward Lucy. Between that green tractor and me, we managed to get Lucy back to the barn.

Edward waited for me to bring Lucy over. Then he closed one of the gates and limped to the house. His knees were bleeding. I walked to the other barn to close the other gate.

As I walked toward the house, I noticed Carrie's car at the driveway. Inside, I found her helping Edward clean his bruised and bloodied knees in the living room. "Hey, stranger!" she exclaimed, getting up to give me a welcoming hug. We talked briefly about my trip as she finished cleaning Edward's injured knees.

He and I then explained how he had gotten hurt. Carrie didn't say much in response, but she shook her head. This was apparently a familiar scene. Edward often got into trouble on the farm.

Once they were done, I headed to the bathroom to take a shower. It had been a long day.

We talked about my trip to New York City over dinner. The Novaks all seemed to be impressed by many of my stories.

After dinner, Carrie sat down at the kitchen table and said, "Santiago, before you go to bed, we have something to ask you."

I nodded and took a seat as she summoned Edward from the other room. A lot of the Novaks' communication occurred through raising their voices to call each other from across the house, and this was no different: she hollered Edward's name, and he came limping into the room. Carrie then called out, "Hey, Macy, do you still have your driver's license manual?" Macy had been studying to get her learner's permit and had been taking lessons at a driving school in preparation for her upcoming test.

Macy was sitting in the living room, watching an episode of *Friends*, and responded with a simple, "Yup."

"Are you done with it?"

"Yeah."

"Could you please bring it to the table? Santiago needs it," Carrie said. This was clearly more of an order than a request.

"Yeah, whatever," Macy mumbled loudly enough for us to hear her.

"I need what?" I asked Edward and Carrie, surprised by this turn of events.

"We thought you could take the driving test tomorrow," Edward said.

Tomorrow?! I thought, slightly panicking. "What for?"

"For our trip to California. This way, if something happens, we'll have an extra driver," Carrie said. The Novaks had previously planned a road trip to California that summer. They thought it would be a good way to show me that part of the country. But now, I had less than fourteen hours to study the Iowa driver's manual and learn to drive a vehicle I had never driven before. And it was all "just in case."

"Okay. I'll get to studying then," I said surprisingly calmly. I grabbed the manual and headed to my room.

Carrie quickly added, "Santiago, fill out these forms, too." She handed me a stack of forms she'd picked up at the Iowa Department of Transportation in Cedar Rapids that day.

My father had taught me how to drive when I was fourteen, so I wasn't particularly worried about the driving portion. One winter weekend, we took his 1994 Volkswagen Beetle to Camaná. Many parts of this beach town were empty during winter, as most of its summer visitors were gone for the season. We drove through Camaná's empty streets for hours as my father taught me the intricacies of driving a manual transmission vehicle. After that, my parents occasionally allowed me to drive around Arequipa. That way, I would have plenty of practice and would be ready for the driving test when I turned eighteen.

I was, however, terrified about taking the written portion of the test. I read the driving manual straight through three times that night and memorized all the signs. I repeated definitions to myself as if I were learning a new language. By the time I fell asleep, I thought I had studied enough to have at least a chance of passing.

The next morning, Edward drove Macy and me to the DOT office in Cedar Rapids so we could both take our tests. There was a long line, so I had some more time to study.

"Why are you studying?" Macy asked.

"Considering that I just got this book last night, I'm nervous," I said.

"I'm not worried," Macy said with all the confidence of a fourteen-year-old, rolling her eyes.

When it was finally our turn, a police officer came out of a back room and called our names. Macy and I walked into a small room that contained several testing computers. Each tester was assigned to a different computer. We could choose to take the test in different languages, including Spanish, but I took the test in English, as the manual I'd used to study was in that language. We had thirty minutes to answer the twenty questions. If you missed four questions, you would fail the test.

While Macy took about fifteen minutes to finish the examination, it took me almost the entire thirty minutes. By the time I got to the final question, I had missed three. So of course, I had no idea what the correct answer to the final question was. Everything hung in the balance, so I did the only thing I could with a multiple-choice test: I guessed and picked answer "C." Luckily, I passed. I walked out of the room, smiling about my good fortune.

"Where's Macy?" I asked Edward, not seeing her with him.

"She's outside, on the phone with Carrie. She didn't pass," Edward said, clearly disappointed.

"So now what?"

"Well, let's see if you can pass the driving test," Edward answered with a wink.

As we walked outside, I saw that the Novaks' four-door Nissan was parked next to a few police cars. A police officer called my name and asked me a few questions to confirm she had the right person. After she verified the paperwork, we climbed into the Nissan. I took the driver's seat and put on my seatbelt. This would be my first time driving this vehicle. "No big deal, Santiago," I whispered to myself.

"I'm sorry, what did you say?" the police officer asked.

"Oh! Nothing, nothing," I said as I tried to figure out how to start the car.

"Sir, put the key in the ignition," she said calmly. "Don't be nervous. It's okay."

I laughed—still nervously—put the key in the ignition, and looked for the clutch. There was no clutch. I looked down at the driving stick and saw that instead of numbers, it had letters. *What's this?* I thought, alarmed.

"Sir, is there a problem?"

"Where are the numbers?" I asked, becoming increasingly worried.

"What numbers?"

"You know: one, two, three. Where is the third pedal?" None of this made sense.

"Sir, have you ever driven a vehicle with an automatic transmission?"

"No, I don't think I have," I said, looking down in defeat. I assumed she would end the test right then and there.

"My goodness. Look, don't tell anyone I said this, but 'D' is for 'Drive.' Once you put it on 'D,' it drives forward, like a go-cart. The left pedal is the brake, and the right one is to accelerate. 'R' is to put it in reverse. Same concept for the pedals. 'P' is for 'Park.' Make sense?" she asked. She really should have stopped the test, but she didn't. I think she felt sorry for me.

"Yes. Thank you."

I turned on the car, put it in drive, and proceeded with the driving test. After we finished, I noticed that I was sweating profusely. The police officer complimented my driving. Thirty minutes later, I received my first driver's license.

I was thrilled. Not everyone, however, was as thrilled as I was.

"I can't believe you passed. This is so unfair," Macy said, physically displaying her disappointment by shaking her head.

Edward drove us back to the house. Macy remained silent the whole way back. I didn't dare mention my awkward driving experience for fear of upsetting my younger host sister even more.

I didn't end up driving during our trip to California. In fact, except for during my driving test, I didn't get behind the wheel once while I was an exchange student.

Chapter Twenty-Eight
THAT TRIP TO CALIFORNIA

July 12, 2000

Our road trip to California taught me three important things about the United States: the importance of corn to the American economy and way of life, the fact that there were seasonal and undocumented workers in the United States, and the notion that many of those working in the retail, food, and lodging businesses spoke Spanish.

Not everyone in the Novak family went on this trip. Edward, Carrie, Macy, and I were the only ones who drove to California. Heather and James stayed in Mount Vernon. It took us two days to drive from Mount Vernon to San Diego, our final destination. On the first day, we drove through Iowa, Nebraska, and Colorado, and although we drove through the cities of Des Moines and Omaha before arriving in Denver, it took us no more than twenty minutes to drive through each city. Des Moines and Omaha had a few tall buildings, but they didn't compare to the skyscrapers I had just seen in New York. I wasn't too interested in learning more about those cities anyway. Although Des Moines and Omaha would become important cities in my future, at the time, I was more interested in the landscape around us.

We had driven for more than four hours, and the landscape hadn't changed. It was all fields of corn on both sides of the road for as far as my eyes could see. Curious, I posed Edward a question: "Who eats all of this corn?"

"What do you mean?"

"I mean, where does it go? There aren't enough people in Iowa and Nebraska to eat it all," I said.

"This corn isn't for eating. It's going to be processed."

"What do you mean by 'processed'?" When I thought about corn, I imagined eating corn on the cob. In Iowa, corn on the cob was sweet and often served covered with a thin layer of butter for additional flavor. In Peru, the kernels were generally larger, but weren't as sweet. Most Peruvians accompanied their corn with small chunks of cheese on the side. I had no idea what "processed" corn was.

"Most of the corn you see will be used as livestock feed," he said. "The rest will be processed and used in products like corn starch, sweeteners, cooking oil, pop, and even fuel."

"Wait, corn in pop?"

"Yes. In fact, most carbonated drinks contain high-fructose corn syrup."

"What's that?" I asked.

"A sweetener made from corn starch."

My jaw dropped. Up to that point, I had thought that all sugars came from sugar cane. "And what do you mean by fuel? Do cars run on corn?" I asked. That seemed even more ridiculous.

"Not exactly, but we have the technology to produce ethanol from corn. Ethanol can be blended with gasoline, so you can use it in cars."

Everything about this conversation was defying conventional wisdom for me. Sweeteners, cooking oil, and even fuel could be made with corn? "You also said that corn is used as livestock feed. That's a lot of corn for animals," I observed.

"Well, pretty soon, you'll understand why we need that much corn for animals. Plus, keep in mind that we export a lot of it," Edward said.

"To where?"

"Mexico and Canada are big markets, though I've heard that China will be a major player in the next few years."

I pondered this for a while. Although I knew that Iowa was a big corn producer, up to then, I didn't know where it all went. Most importantly, I certainly didn't know that corn-based products were everywhere.

Soon, the landscape started to change, and cornfields were replaced by pastures. The number of cows I saw seemed to grow exponentially as we drove west. Edward took a small detour and drove us to a strange place I hadn't even imagined existed: a feedlot.

One of Edward's childhood friends ran a feedlot operation in western Nebraska. This friend had started his business with about ten cows, but in a few years, he had grown his operation to around one thousand head. Edward's friend was kind enough to let us observe his feeding operation, but he said that we couldn't spend too much time there. When we walked over to the feedlot, I understood why: the unmistakable smell of manure was so strong, that it was difficult to handle.

I had never seen anything like it before, and although I wanted to ask many questions, I didn't say much. Instead, I simply observed, as I usually did when faced with new experiences. This seemed like a vast operation to me, but I heard Edward's friend mention that this was actually a rather small operation and that he had been thinking about selling it to a corporate farmer.

Before I moved to Mount Vernon, I thought farmers were simply individuals who owned land and decided to farm on it. My understanding of farming was limited to small—and for the most part, poor—family farms in Peru. In Iowa, I learned about the concept of corporations owning farms, and how farming could be a lucrative business.

"Santiago, do you understand why we need that much corn now? There are a lot of cattle to feed," Edward said as we looked out at the feedlot.

There were indeed. I couldn't believe that there was a place on earth solely dedicated to feeding cattle. Edward explained that the purpose of these places was to feed cattle before sending them to slaughterhouses. Generally, prior to entering a feedlot, cattle would spend their lives grazing in pastures. Once they reached a certain weight—usually when they turned one year old—they were sent to feedlots. Edward wasn't okay with this practice, as he preferred a more humane method of treating animals. He was also concerned about the environmental contamination caused by those operations, but he understood that many small-town economies depended on them.

Before we left, Edward's friend also said something that caught my attention: he thought it was great that I knew how to speak Spanish, as it was a valuable skill in his business. When I asked why, he explained that many meat-packing plants hire seasonal migrant workers from Mexico and

Central America. Most Americans don't want to work these types of jobs, as they are tough and dirty. As a result, the workforce largely comes from Spanish-speaking countries, so a worker's ability to speak both Spanish and English is highly valued. If that worker was also documented, he or she was even more valuable.

Documented workers? Migrant workers? Seasonal jobs? Apparently, I still had so much to learn about this country, and I had too many unanswered questions.

One thing had become clear, though: corn was vital to Nebraska's and Iowa's economies. Ever since I started to understand English, I heard people in Iowa talk about being "corn-fed." As we continued to drive west, that concept started to make sense: corn was everywhere and in everything.

As we got back in the car and continued to head west into Colorado, the landscape changed even more. The flat fields started to become bumpy. Soon, mountains appeared on the horizon. We drove through Denver and on into the mountains.

That night, we stopped in a small Colorado mountain town for dinner and found a motel next to a truck stop. I didn't sleep much though, as I could hear people walking around outside all night. The motel reminded me of those you'd see in American movies where someone was usually murdered. The murderer had easy access to the rooms, and the victims couldn't escape. Luckily, we made it through the night unharmed.

In the morning, we continued our trip west. On the second day, we drove through the rest of Colorado, Utah, Nevada, and California, all the way to San Diego. We drove through Las Vegas, but we didn't stop there—alas, I have no fun Sin City stories to tell.

In San Diego, we stayed with Edward's cousin Nancy. She had moved to California from Iowa in the mid-seventies for college and never moved back. As she explained it, "I endured enough harsh winters for a lifetime." I could certainly relate to the sentiment. Nancy lived in a wealthy neighborhood in a beautiful two-level house with a large backyard and a beautifully manicured front yard. She was a kind, good-natured person.

When we arrived, we were all tired from the long drive and quickly went to sleep. I wanted to stay up and talk to Nancy, but I could barely keep my eyes open.

I woke up early the next morning. After a quick shower, I walked into the living room. I didn't find anyone, so I looked around and admired some fascinating oil paintings on the walls.

"Good morning, Santiago," Nancy called through the back door. She had been sitting outside on the patio, reading, and having a glass of freshly squeezed orange juice. She had an orange tree in her fenced backyard and took advantage of it whenever she could. Her home was at the top of a hill, and she had a stunning view of the city from her patio.

I joined her outside. "Good morning. This is a great view," I remarked.

"Thanks. Want some orange juice?"

"Of course," I responded.

As I sipped my juice, I walked over to the orange tree and noticed that there were several oranges ready to be picked. I also noticed some people fixing the neighbor's roof. I was surprised to realize that they were speaking Spanish.

"What are they saying?" Nancy asked when she noticed I was looking at the workers.

"They're talking about soccer," I responded casually. I had overheard them talk about Necaxa, a Mexican soccer team.

"I can never understand them. Sometimes I think they're talking about me," she said.

"Do a lot of people speak Spanish around here?" I asked.

She laughed and explained that most of the "labor" in the area spoke Spanish. One could find Spanish-speaking people at most restaurants, stores, hotels, cleaning companies, roofing companies, and landscaping companies. If you needed some kind of manual labor, you better have some knowledge of Spanish. Many workers spoke English, too, but for the most part, Spanish was their native tongue. "We have a lot of people who cross the border for work. Some legally, some illegally. They get paid better here. Can you blame them?" she asked.

Since I was new to the whole immigration debate, I didn't know how to respond. Aside from Alberto and Emilia, no one else in my family had ever immigrated to the United States. I knew that some of my friends had traveled to the United States for vacation, but they always returned to Peru. Moreover, Nancy was referring to the Mexico-United States border in her comments, and I didn't know anyone who had crossed that border. "Do people who cross the border, legally or illegally, usually stay?" I asked.

"Not always, but many do. It's complicated." After a pause, she added, "You know, I could use your help. My landscaper is working on the front yard right now. I've been trying to tell him not to trim some plants, but he keeps trimming them. He doesn't speak much English. Can you help me?"

Although this request may have been awkward to some, I didn't think much of it. I knew how to speak Spanish, so I was glad to help. "Sure," I said.

We walked around to the front of the house, and Nancy introduced me to Juan, her landscaper. Juan was a short, stocky man who was probably in his mid-forties. His sun-damaged skin and tired appearance contrasted with his warm smile and positive attitude.

I told Juan, in Spanish, that Nancy had some comments about his work and that she wanted him to fix some of the landscaping. He listened to me carefully and took some notes. Then he called out to a boy—he couldn't have been older than fourteen or so—who had been working on the lawn as well. Apparently, this was Juan's son, and he was part of the family business. As the boy came toward us, I asked Juan where he was from, just to make conversation.

"Guatemala, sir," he said timidly.

"Do you live in California permanently?"

He looked down and asked his son to bring the lawnmower. It appeared that he didn't want to answer the question. After a brief moment of hesitation, he looked into my eyes. "Why do you ask?" he asked in a subtly defiant tone.

"I'm sorry, Juan. I didn't mean to pry. I was just curious. I'm from Peru, and I'm an exchange student in Iowa. This is my first time in California, and I've seen a lot of people speaking Spanish here," I said, attempting to smooth over any feathers I had accidentally ruffled.

"I live here, sir," he said.

"Okay, Juan. I'm sorry. Again, I didn't mean to pry."

Juan looked down again. I could tell that he felt uncomfortable, and I decided to end our conversation. I walked away, waved at him and his son, and went back into the house. I felt embarrassed for asking him such questions, but I also wondered why he hesitated to answer.

Growing up in Peru, I was never exposed to people "crossing the border" for work and never had to cross any border myself for anything other than vacations and sporting events. I didn't have to worry about immigration issues in my Peruvian bubble. Unlike Juan's son, I didn't have to work. If I learned anything from my awkward and uncomfortable interaction with Juan, it's that I needed to be more sensitive to other people's circumstances. A question about nationality or residency may not mean much for some, but for many, like Juan, it may feel like someone is trying to question their legal status. Although I didn't mean to make him uncomfortable, I now see how he might have thought that he was being racially or ethnically profiled. I now understand how that innocent exchange may have seemed like an interrogation for him and that he may have thought that Nancy had sent me to ask him those questions. Although we shared the same language and perhaps the same interests—like Latin music and soccer—we didn't share the same nationality, the same traditions, or the same background. My conversation with Juan sparked my desire to learn more about people from other Latin American countries living in this country—not only about other cultural traditions and idiosyncrasies, but also about how their struggles and successes have shaped the United States. That conversation was the beginning of a long quest to understand my place in this country. About twenty years later, I am still trying to find it.

Inside, Nancy thanked me for discussing the landscaping issue with Juan. By then, Edward and Carrie were up, and they were having breakfast. "Santiago, what did you talk about with Juan?" Nancy asked.

"I just wanted to know more about him and asked him whether he lived here permanently," I said.

"Oh. Did he respond?" she asked. She seemed surprised that I had asked such a question.

"Yes, but I don't think he wanted to. Our conversation was awkward."

"He probably wasn't expecting that kind of question from you. He's very private about such things," she explained gently.

"Do you know much about him?"

"Not much. Another neighbor recommended him to me. He does good work at a fair price. It's hard to find help like that around here," she said simply. She had been told that Juan did good work and that he was an honest guy. She trusted her friend's advice and didn't think twice about hiring him.

I didn't ask any more questions about Juan. I did wonder about his son, though: a boy who looked like a younger version of me. At his age, I spent my summer months at a modest beach house that my family rented for the season. This boy had to help his father put food on the table by mowing other people's lawns. This was just another reminder of the economic disparities in the world.

*   *   *

Over the next few days, we did all the popular touristy things: we went to Disneyland, SeaWorld, and the beach. We also visited several wealthy neighborhoods to admire the lavish homes of the rich and famous. Although I felt a bit out of place because I assumed I would never be able to afford a home in such a wealthy neighborhood, I was grateful that we were able to visit those places. They represented the perfectly manicured United States I had only seen in the movies.

Before we left California, we took a trip to Big Bear Lake, a small town on Bear Mountain in Southern California known for its ski resort. During the winter, the town is filled with tourists who spend their days skiing, shopping, and enjoying the local restaurants. In the summer, this vacation destination still offers hiking trails, water activities, and—of course—restaurants and shopping. We went there because Marco, a friend of mine from Peru, was working there for the summer. In Peru, Marco had attended a high school with an intensive English program, so he was fluent in it. He was a year older than me, and this was his second year working at the resort.

We arrived at Big Bear Lake in the morning. Marco couldn't meet us in the morning, but he was free in the afternoon, so Edward, Carrie, Macy, and I used the morning to explore the town. When Marco finished his shift, he met up with us, and I introduced him to my host family.

I was curious about his work at the resort. I had heard that Peruvian students often traveled to the United States at certain times of the year to work for a few months. Students could apply for seasonal jobs at resorts by obtaining a J1 Visa, a document that allowed them to live and work in the United States for a limited period of time. The students would then perform inexpensive labor for the resorts while getting some unique international work experience.

Marco introduced me to a few of his co-workers. Most were college students who worked at the resort for a few months at a time. Although many considered the job simply a way to make some extra money, for many of them, the money they earned during the summer would pay for many of their necessities back home. This was a fascinating world, and I had so many questions about it. I was surprised to find that not only were Edward and Carrie unaware of the student work visa program, they also didn't seem to care much about it. I did.

Our time in California flew by, and before we knew it, we had to drive back to Iowa. Although I had learned a lot during this trip, I felt that many of my questions remained unanswered. I had discovered an entire world I hadn't known existed—something that seemed to be a regular part of my life at this point.

Our drive back to Iowa seemed to take even longer than our initial drive out to California. Edward and Carrie shared driving duties again. I tried to converse with them as much as I could, mostly because I wanted to make sure they wouldn't fall asleep, but also because I wanted to learn more. We talked about politics a lot, and with so much time on our hands, we were able to cover a lot of ground. Among other things, we discussed immigration, undocumented workers, the military, social security, the National Rifle Association, abortion issues, the presidential elections, and discrimination in the United States.

I already knew that the Novaks held a conservative view on most political issues, and while I agreed with them on some things, we disagreed on others. We never argued to the point of contention, though, and we were willing to listen to each other. That by itself seemed to be more than most people were willing to do at the time.

Chapter Twenty-Nine
MOVING INTO TOWN

August 11, 2000

A few weeks after my California trip, it was time for me to move into a new home. Most exchange student programs require their students to live with a few different host families during the course of their stay, and the Rotary exchange program was no different. I would be moving in with the Petersons.

Unlike the Novaks, who lived on a farm, the Petersons lived in town. Although I had enjoyed my experience at the farm and the Novaks had been wonderful to me, I was ready for something different. It was time for me to leave the farm behind.

Kenneth Peterson picked me up from the Novaks' home. Since this wasn't a permanent goodbye, no one cried or appeared too saddened by my move. Edward helped me with my bags while Carrie made sure I hadn't forgotten anything in my room.

Once we put my bags in Kenneth's SUV, I jumped in the front seat.

"Hungry, Santiago?" he asked. I liked him instantly. He seemed like a typical Iowa parent. He wore jeans, white tennis shoes, white socks, and a polo shirt. Yet there was something about him that caught my attention. It didn't take me long to realize that it was because we had a similar sense of humor.

"Yes, I am. Do you have a place in mind?" I asked.

"Want to grab some wings?"

"Sure," I said.

We drove to a sports bar for lunch. As we walked in, I noticed about five televisions surrounding the bar. Each table had a metal bucket containing mustard, ketchup, and hot sauce. We ordered chicken wings while watching the replay of a previous year's football game on one of the large-screen TVs. We made some small talk, and I asked about my new host mom. Kenneth said that she had gone to the school to fill out some paperwork, officially changing my "home" address to theirs and listing them as my new emergency contacts. She would meet us at home later.

I immediately noticed a stark difference between my host fathers. While Edward was high-strung and expressive, Kenneth was calm and collected. Edward was a farmer, while Kenneth was an insurance agent. There was a certain sophistication to the way Kenneth spoke that I found appealing. He reminded me of a younger version of Harrison Ford, whom I had seen in dubbed movies back home. Both Edward and Kenneth would turn out to be positive influences in my life, each in his own unique way.

After a few jokes and a few chicken wings, we drove to my new home. Although the Petersons lived in town, their house was close to a creek and surrounded by trees. It was almost like it was within its own small forest. The house was a ranch-style home, and my bedroom was in the basement next to the television room and across from a small office. The basement had a door that led out to the small forest. Unlike my room at the Novaks' place, I didn't find any deer heads, rifles, or dream catchers. I did encounter a couple of fishing poles hidden inside the closet and a bunch of hunting magazines, though.

As I started unpacking my clothes, Linda, my new host mother, came into my room and introduced herself. She asked me to let her know if I needed anything. I thanked her, as I was still struggling to organize my bedroom.

After a couple of hours of organizing, I headed upstairs to grab something to drink. I poured myself a glass of water and wandered around the house, looking for the Petersons. They were outside. Linda was gardening, and Kenneth was in the garage, cleaning his hunting rifles and hanging out with their dog, Max, a beautiful and docile golden retriever.

I'm something of a dog person, so I had an instant connection with Max. I grabbed one of his toys and played with him for a while. "Want to take Max for a walk?" Kenneth asked, noticing my interest.

"Sure," I responded.

"Linda, we're going on a walk with the dog," Kenneth said as he put his guns in a safe. Linda nodded and waved as we set out.

Kenneth allowed me to take Max's leash as we took a stroll around town. Although I had lived in Mount Vernon for several months, I had never seen this part of town before. We walked by several larger-than-average homes, most of them with meticulously maintained front yards. Clearly, the Petersons lived in the wealthy part of town.

This walk was typical for Kenneth, but it was far from ordinary for me. When I was younger, I often watched American movies and television and fantasized about one day living in what I considered to be a "traditional" American suburb: a place full of large homes with two-car garages, driveways, large front yards, and plenty of room for kids to play. In my mind, and in the minds of many of my Peruvian friends, that image of a privileged American suburb was what we aspired to: picket fences, expensive cars, and people wearing fancy clothes. However, I had also always assumed that those kinds of neighborhoods were reserved for movie stars and rich people. They weren't for me. Although I had grown up as part of the Peruvian middle class, our home and neighborhood were modest. Living in the Petersons' neighborhood was a unique experience for me.

When we returned to the house, Kenneth and I joined Linda for a quick mid-afternoon snack. We talked about our walk, and Linda asked me about my recent trips to New York and California. I felt comfortable with them and shared some of my experiences.

As we chatted at the kitchen table, I noticed the loving manner in which Kenneth looked at Linda. Kenneth was in his early fifties, and they had been married for almost thirty years, but he still looked at her as if they were two young lovers. They had fun together. They laughed and shared their thoughts. At that moment, I realized that I had moved into the home of a happy and successful marriage.

In the years leading up to my trip to Iowa, my parents hadn't gotten along well. My father had been traveling often for work, which fueled the growing anger and resentment between them. After a very unfortunate event that caused a lot of pain to my family—the details of which I will keep out of this book—my father left our home and moved into a small apartment by himself. At that point, my parents had officially separated.

The day my father left our home, I'd been studying for a history test in my bedroom when he asked me to join him. I walked into his office with him, and we talked. We had a difficult and tense discussion about the unfortunate event that had transpired over the past few days and ended up breaking my parent's marriage. After our talk, he left the house for good. I had just turned sixteen.

After that talk with my father, I walked into my brother's bedroom and sat down next to him. He was asleep. He was only eleven years old, so I didn't wake him up to tell him what had just happened. Instead, I gave him a kiss on the forehead and went to my room. I closed the door, grabbed my Walkman, and listened to some music. I cried for hours before falling asleep.

The next morning, at school, I couldn't focus. How could I? My mind was still on the conversation of the previous night. The history test I had been studying for was scheduled for third period, and I was far from prepared for it. I tried to study during my first two classes, but it was impossible. I felt defeated.

Minutes before my test, Manolo, a Catholic priest who had become my spiritual mentor at the high school, stopped by my classroom and asked the teacher to excuse me for a few minutes. My mother had called him to let him know what had transpired at home. In many ways, Manolo was more than a spiritual mentor; he was also a friend. I would often stop by his office during recess just to talk. He knew that I needed to talk now more than ever.

Inside his office, Manolo asked me to take a seat and to tell him what had happened during my conversation with my father. I struggled to speak, but was eventually able to get it out. After that, he asked me how I felt. I couldn't say anything. I had shut down, and it was apparent.

He opened one of his desk drawers and pulled out a wooden ruler. "Break it," he said, handing it to me.

"What? Why?"

"Trust me. Break it," he repeated.

I grabbed the wooden ruler and bent it until it broke in two pieces. At that moment, a rush of emotions overwhelmed me, and I started crying uncontrollably. Manolo gave me a hug and said that I could stay in his office as long as I wanted. I spent a couple of hours there with him before heading back to class. I was upset, and I needed time to process things.

Before I left his office, Manolo asked me, "Does your brother know?"

"Joaquin? I don't know. I don't think so."

"You must look after him. If this was hard for you, it'll be even harder for him. He's young and vulnerable," he explained. I took his words to heart.

That afternoon, when I got home from school, I found my mother crying. I asked her what had happened, and she said that Joaquin knew our father had left. I hurried to his room and found my brother lying on his bed quietly. I hugged him and asked him to go for a walk with me. He agreed.

I went to the backyard to get our dog, Cooper, a beautiful and mischievous white Samoyed. This dog had been with me through it all, and I felt that he needed to be with us now.

The three of us walked to a park a block away. As I started to ask him how he felt, my brother suddenly burst into tears. I hugged him and cried with him. "It'll be okay, we'll be okay," I kept telling him. We sat down right in the middle of the park, with Cooper sitting between us. I held Joaquin until he stopped crying, which took some time. After that, we walked back to the house. I turned on the television and asked him to play video games with me, something I hadn't done in a while. At that moment, I made a promise to myself: I would always look after Joaquin.

In Mount Vernon, seeing the Petersons interact in such loving manner made me think about my parents. Although they never fought in front of us, I couldn't remember them ever displaying that kind of affection. Hence, I was intrigued by the Petersons' relationship. I wanted to know how they had managed to stay together for so many years and still show that kind of affection for each other. I needed to learn how a couple lived in a successful marriage.

I have a good feeling about this place, I thought.

Chapter Thirty
WHAT ABOUT THOSE TITANS?

September 29, 2000

Kenneth thought that going to the movies would be a good way to start the weekend, and he was looking forward to seeing a new release. He'd heard that it had gotten great reviews, and because of the underlying theme of the movie, he thought it was an important movie for me to see. It was called *Remember the Titans*.

Based on a true story, *Remember the Titans* portrayed the efforts of a football coach to integrate an all-white high school football team in Virginia in 1971. The coaching staff included a black head coach and a white assistant coach who ended up working together to unite a group of black and white students to play as a team. It portrayed many of the struggles that American families encountered as they lived through the integration of American schools. To me, it was a revelation, as it was hard to believe that schools were ever segregated, let alone that segregation had ended only about thirty years before I moved to the United States.

What wasn't a revelation was Americans' passion for football, a sport I'd never even thought about playing until I'd tried out for the high school team a few weeks earlier.

I didn't grow up playing football. I played *fútbol* instead, the name that soccer goes by in the rest of the world. So when my friend David asked me to try out for the high school football team, I hesitated. "David, I've never played before," I told him.

"Don't worry, Santiago. You're fast and can kick a ball. You can be the kicker or part of special teams," he assured me.

"But I don't even know the rules."

"Don't worry, I'll teach you," he said. It was early August, and the school year had not yet started, so I was hanging out at his house. He cleaned off a dry-erase board that he usually used for homework and spent about an hour explaining the many different positions and rules of the game. The game was way more complicated than I'd thought. He talked about downs, passes, punts, touchdowns, and field goals. He said that each team had a quarterback, offensive linemen, wide receivers, running backs, fullbacks, tight ends, defensive linemen, defensive tackles, defensive ends, linebackers, safeties, and kickers. I felt like I needed to learn a new language just to understand the game.

"Have you ever kicked a football?" he asked then.

"No, but how hard can it be? I can kick a soccer ball pretty well," I quipped.

David laughed and explained that kicking a football wasn't as simple as kicking a soccer ball. A soccer ball is spherical, which means there's a certain amount of predictability about where the ball goes. A football is a "prolate spheroid," a fancy term for the shape of a pig's inflated bladder. When kicked, if not kicked correctly, it can move in several different directions. "Don't worry, though," David reassured me. "We'll have plenty of time to practice."

That night, he gave me a small book with all the rules and different plays. I tried to study it, but it was difficult. There were too many rules, positions, and plays to memorize.

About fifty players attended the first practice. Some of them were also on the soccer team, so I stayed close to them. Coach Crawford opened the first practice by giving a short speech. "Welcome back to those who played last year. To those who are new, especially those who played other sports before, like soccer, welcome to the *real* football team," he said with a raspy voice. Coach Crawford was a stocky middle-aged man with bright white hair and a belly.

I wondered about his comments for a moment. The *real* football team? Why was it "real" football? Thus far, from what I had read and seen, this kind of football was mostly played with one's hands, not one's feet. In fact, except for the kicker, most players didn't play the sport with their feet at all. *Maybe since "handball" was already taken, they were stuck with the next best thing when naming the sport,* I thought.

After Coach's speech, we warmed up and then got in a line behind the assistant coach. The coaches had set up different stations to help them calculate our agility, test our leg power, grade our sprint speed, and measure our throwing and receiving skills. I did well on the agility and speed exercises, average on the receiving tests, and depressingly poorly on the leg power and throwing exercises. I quickly realized that David's assessment was correct: I wasn't going to be the quarterback, nor did I have the body of a linebacker. Special teams would be my bread and butter.

After practice, David drove me home. I took a shower, went to my room, and studied the rule book some more.

Until the school year started, we had practice in the morning. David gave me a ride to practice again the next day. We had become close friends. "What are we doing today?" I asked as I climbed into his car. This was his fourth year playing football, so he knew the schedule well.

"We'll hit each other," he said simply.

"We'll do what?"

"Don't worry. The coaches will show us how to hit, so you won't break your neck."

"Perfect," I whispered.

Coach gave us another of his succinct speeches that morning. This time, he tried to motivate us by slowly instilling fear in our minds: fear of making mistakes, of not giving one hundred percent in every practice. It worked: I was ready to push people around. Or so I thought.

Before heading to the practice field, we walked to the cafeteria so the coaches could get our height and weight. I clocked in at 5'10" and 155 pounds. I definitely wasn't the biggest guy of the team. In Peru, in the nineties, strength training wasn't common, so most Peruvian high school athletes were thin. I was no exception.

After we got our measurements, we went to the locker room to pick up our practice gear. I was given a helmet, shoulder pads, a couple of shirts and shorts, and some kind of protective underwear. I examined it curiously, and David chimed in: "You better wear that. You don't want to get hurt in that area."

"I don't want to get hurt at all," I muttered.

I had never worn football gear before, so David helped me put the shoulder pads on. It wasn't comfortable. Once we had changed into our equipment, we walked out to the field.

The coaches separated the team into two lines. One line included the bigger players, while the other line—my line—had the smaller guys. Then, they paired us up: a bigger player with a smaller player. I was paired with Dani, one of the tallest and biggest guys on the team. Next, the coaches separated all the pairs into three different groups to complete three different exercises. The first exercise involved running around cones. I beat Dani every time. For the second exercise, we had to sprint forty yards, five times. Again, it was no contest.

For the third and last exercise, we had to tackle each other. One of the assistant coaches walked us through the process: "Stay low, sink the hips, heads up, and tackle using your shoulder." He demonstrated the correct way to tackle. It looked simple enough. "Hands up, wrap up, and grab a piece of clothing. Move your feet, so you're not caught flat-footed," he added. Then it was our turn.

I stood in front of a mat with Dani directly in front of me. He was about 6'3" and 230 pounds. He had a kind face, but knowing that he was about to hit me made him seem intimidating.

"Set… go," our assistant coach shouted.

Dani bent his knees, moved forward, and tackled me. That tackle was the equivalent of having a chiropractor adjust my joints all at one time. My entire body shook and cracked like never before.

When it was my turn to tackle him, I bent my knees and tackled Dani as hard as I could. I bounced right off him. I think that tackle hurt me more than it hurt him.

We repeated the exercise a few times, always with the same result: me falling on my back, hurting a different part of my body, and starting to think that I was damaging internal organs with every hit.

When practice was over, David took me home, and after a very long shower, I immediately fell asleep. The next morning, I woke up feeling like I'd been run over by a train. That feeling continued for days.

Although I tried hard in every practice, Coach wasn't fond of me because I had played soccer. He didn't like soccer because the soccer team used the football fields to practice, and our cleats tore it up. However, he knew I could sprint, so he put me on some special teams and had me play as a wide receiver. Despite that, I had never caught a ball during a play, as the quarterback never threw it to me.

Then, one rainy afternoon, Coach wasn't happy about the way practice had been going and asked our quarterback to throw the ball wide, to the wide receivers, more often. At the huddle, our quarterback asked me to run five yards to the left, make a ninety-degree turn, run ten yards, and then turn to him. Since the ball had never ended up in my hands before, I went through the motions as he asked without thinking that I would actually need to catch it. However, when I turned to the quarterback, I saw the ball coming straight at me like a dart.

I could catch well, so that wasn't a problem. The problem arose when I turned to run with it. As soon as I began to sprint, I noticed several helmets from the other team furiously coming toward me. Before getting tackled, I experienced something I had never experienced before on a field: I feared for my life. That experience could only be compared to the feeling of getting mugged. And unfortunately, *that* was a feeling I'd experienced a couple of times back in Peru. I faked a couple of players and kept running until I felt someone hit my left leg. I felt a stabbing pain in my knee and dropped to the ground. Our quarterback ran toward me, offered me a hand, and told me "Good job." My knee hurt, but I tried to shake it off.

After that play, Coach asked all the kickers to join the special teams and get ready to kick some field goals. The rain started to fall heavily then, and I told an assistant coach that it was getting too slippery to kick. He said I shouldn't worry about it, as we only had a few plays left.

Coach set up the teams to kick field goals. Although I was hurting a bit, I was ready to kick the football. During this play, someone would throw the ball to the player kneeling in front of the kicker. They would grab it and place it on the ground for them to kick. Unfortunately, on one of those "few plays left," after I kicked the ball, a player from the other team slipped and fell. He crashed into me and landed on my knee. This time, I felt a cracking sensation. I had torn my meniscus. Although it was a small tear, I was not allowed to practice contact sports for a while. My football season was over before it had even begun.

Although I never actually played in a football game, I went to most of my high school's games and enjoyed the experience. I loved how the entire town religiously congregated at the stadium on Friday nights to celebrate and support its team. The whole experience seemed like something out of a movie. It was just like the football season in *Remember the Titans*—minus the extreme racial tensions, of course.

The film's depiction of racism and segregation in the United States seemed unreal. I found myself wondering, *Did that really happen? Was there really a time when black and white students couldn't go to the same school?* According to the movie, there was, and it wasn't all that long ago.

In Peru, I had done one presentation on the United States Declaration of Independence for my history class. For my presentation, I memorized—in Spanish, of course—parts of the Declaration, including the second paragraph: "We hold these truths to be self-evident, that all men are created equal, that they are endowed by their Creator with certain unalienable Rights, that among these are Life, Liberty, and the pursuit of Happiness."

If all "men" were created equal, why had blacks and whites been forced to go to different schools? If all Americans had a right to "the pursuit of happiness," did that mean that Americans only had that right so long as they lived their lives with people who look like them?

I knew that I didn't look like most people in Iowa. My skin color was brown. I was different. I wasn't white or black. But why would that matter? Except for the color of my skin and my thick Spanish accent, I was just like everyone else: a human being.

Although I hadn't grown up worrying about the color of my skin, it wasn't because Peru wasn't a divided country; it was because I was on the "right" side on the fence. Peru is a deeply divided country. It's a society where having an aristocratic last name, going to a private school, or even having the "right" skin tone—white or light brown—can determine a person's level of success. Often, it's not about what you know, but about who you know. It's a beautiful country with a rich history and a unique landscape, but with marked inequalities. As absurd as it may sound, since I had gone to a private school and my skin tone was not too dark— it's actually light brown by Peruvian standards—I never had to worry or even think about whether anyone would think less of me because of the color of my skin. I lived in a bubble, and that bubble burst in the United States.

A few months prior to seeing *Remember the Titans*, I had faced discrimination for the first time in my life. At the time, I thought it was simply an isolated incident. However, after traveling to the East and West Coasts and seeing that movie, I started to wonder whether it really was an isolated event. Did it reflect a larger pattern in the United States, and it only happened because someone was finally vocal about their feelings? Unless a person expresses his or her thoughts, it's impossible to know how they really feel about you. I began to wonder whether most Americans thought that the color of a person's skin was actually a relevant factor in the way they interacted with each other. I began to truly wonder what people thought of me.

After *Remember the Titans*, I felt that perhaps I had to be more careful when meeting new people in the United States. Although I didn't want to live in a permanent state of paranoia, I thought it would be good to pay more attention to what people said to me. Even though I didn't like it, I had to remember those Titans.

Chapter Thirty-One
AN UNLIKELY FRIENDSHIP

October 5, 2000

After I moved into town with the Petersons, I made a habit of walking to the local coffee shop a couple of times a week after school to get a healthy dose of caffeine. I would usually order a mocha, sit at a table in the corner, and read a book or magazine. I wanted to learn English well and found that having coffee and spending time in a coffee shop was the perfect set-up for reading.

On one such visit, I noticed two old men sitting at the next table. I had seen them before, as they regularly visited the coffee shop around the same time I did and often sat at the same table. "Hi, you aren't from here, are you?" one of them asked me on this particular day.

My host family had told me to be careful when talking to strangers, but they seemed harmless. "No, I'm from Peru," I told them.

"Peru, Nebraska?" the other one asked.

"Peru, South America."

"Why would you think he's from Nebraska, Earl? Can't you tell he has an accent? You can be so observant sometimes," the first man said. "What's your name? I'm Dean. My sharp friend here is Earl."

"My name's Santiago. Nice to meet you."

"What brings you to Mount Vernon?" Dean asked.

"I'm an exchange student at the high school."

"That sounds interesting. I've never met an exchange student before. Want to join us?" Earl asked.

"Leave the kid alone," Dean said. "What's he going to do with two old fogies like us? Sorry, kid. Keep reading your book."

I was reading a basic English grammar book, and it wasn't exactly interesting. "I don't mind. I could use a break."

"Alrighty then. Pull up your chair," Dean said.

I grabbed my chair and my cup of coffee, put my book in my backpack, and scooted over to sit next to Earl. They asked me about Peru and how I had come to the United States. I gave them a glimpse into my year thus far, although I was far more interested in learning about them. They seemed like an interesting pair. "How did you two meet?" I asked when I had finally satisfied their curiosity.

"We were neighbors. We didn't always like each other, though," Earl said.

"Who said I like you now?" Dean teased.

"Dean, you couldn't live without me."

"Why is it you didn't like each other?" I asked, cutting through the good-natured bickering.

"We liked the same girl," Earl said.

I found it intriguing that some things appeared to be universal. In Peru, when I was younger, my cousin got in a fight with one of his best friends over a girl. They didn't talk to each other for years, even though the girl ended up with someone else entirely. It was peculiar that these two American men disliked each other at one point for the same reason. "Where's the girl now?" I asked.

"She passed away a few years ago," Earl said.

"Oh, I'm sorry," I said, suddenly worried that I had treaded into emotional territory.

"Thank you. It's okay. She lived a full life," Earl said.

"She's the reason why I went to Iowa State," Dean added. I tilted my head to the side in a questioning gesture, and he continued, "During my senior year of high school, I asked her to prom. She said she already had a date: Earl. I was so devastated, I didn't go to my prom."

"How did that make you want to go to Iowa State?" I asked. They could tell I was confused.

"Let me finish. I applied to the University of Iowa and to Iowa State University. I got into both schools, and since my beloved friend here was accepted to the University of Iowa, I chose the other school," Dean explained. In other words, he chose Iowa State because he didn't want to see Earl and his girlfriend in Iowa City.

After they both departed for college, they didn't talk to each other for several years, even though Earl's relationship with the girl they both liked ended during their freshman year. After college, Earl attended law school and worked as a lawyer in Des Moines. Dean became an engineer and moved to California. They didn't keep in touch. Then, about ten years ago, after having successful careers, they both retired and moved back to Mount Vernon and have lived in the same neighborhood ever since.

They met up again at one of those traditional Iowa potluck meals. Earl and his wife brought green bean casserole. Dean and his wife brought apple pie. They sat at the same table and shared stories. After a few minutes, they agreed to leave their fights and disagreements in the past and move on. That's when they agreed to meet at the coffee shop. At first, it was just to catch up, but after a few cups of coffee, they decided to make their meeting a weekly event. Now, their families get together on the weekends, and they spend most holidays as a unit.

"What do you guys talk about?" I asked, intrigued.

"We usually start out talking about our families, and then we move on to sports and politics. During football season, we usually just talk about the Hawkeyes and the Cyclones. This year, however, we've been talking about the election," Dean said.

"I see. Do you have a political affiliation?"

"I'm a registered Republican," Dean said proudly.

"And I'm a registered Democrat," Earl added.

"And you're friends?" I asked. I was surprised. Given what I had seen from some of the media outlets and learned from previous conversations with other Americans, it seemed incredible that a Republican and a Democrat could be such good friends.

"Yes, we're friends. Although we don't agree on everything, we make it work," Dean said.

"I'll be frank, though. I'm not as passionate about the party as I used to be," Earl said.

"How so?"

"I think it's safe to say that we've both moved away from the extremes. I used to be a hard-core Democrat, but I think the country is better off if the parties can at least talk to each other," Earl said.

"I agree. I used to be as conservative as they come," Dean added.

"Why did you change?"

"Because we care more about the future of our country than the future of our politicians," Dean said.

Earl echoed the sentiment: "Amen to that!"

"Anyway, Santiago, you're a kid. Why do you keep asking about politics? Why do you care? Shouldn't you be playing video games or whatever kids your age do these days?" Dean asked.

"I'm in Iowa to learn about the United States. Peru's politics are a mess. I want to learn from this country, so I can take what I learn back home."

"Boy, you're in for a treat. We may have a bigger mess here," Dean said.

I told them that I was interested in learning more about the two main political parties. I couldn't believe that just two major parties had dominated American politics for so long. It seemed like there had to be more than just two ways of thinking about things. In Peru, there are several parties, and although some are the "traditional" ones that run year after year, many are organized for a specific election.

"Fair enough," Dean said. "We'll attempt to give you a glimpse of how we see things happening today."

"Okay. I'll put on my Democrat hat. Can you put on your Republican hat, Dean?"

"My elephant hat is on."

Earl started by saying that the taxes Americans pay should go to building a more efficient government, which in turn would provide better social services to its citizens. He argued that he paid taxes so the government could build better roads, help the poor and the underprivileged, and assist children and the elderly. He didn't mind paying a bit more in taxes so long as children could get a better education and the elderly could get better care. "It's only fair," Earl said.

Dean agreed with Earl in that their taxes must be used for social services; however, he felt that the federal government had become too big and that it needed to be reformed. He argued that personal responsibility, and not government handouts, is the keystone of American society. If the government were smaller and more effective, then Americans would have to pay fewer taxes, allowing more money to remain in the market.

I jumped in to clarify: "Wait, Earl, so you're saying that one party wants the government to help more people, and to do so, it needs to raise taxes, while the other party wants a more effective and smaller government, so the individuals are taxed less?"

"It's a lot more complicated than that, but I can go with that for now," Earl responded.

"I'm sorry, but it seems that, at the core, each party wants to take the country down completely different roads," I said.

"Bingo," Earl said. "The parties of extremes—that's the new game in politics."

"You see, I don't mind if I get taxed a bit more, so long as the government is efficient and it provides fair services," Dean said.

"And I don't mind if we have a smaller government, so long as we don't cut services that people truly need," Earl added.

"We've learned that with our political system, as it stands, we can't have both, so we try to find a way to work things out. But to do so, the parties must listen to and try to understand each other," Dean explained.

"Listen? I think you're asking too much of our politicians, Dean. You know that would be pushing the limits of the impossible."

"And that's why we're worried about the future of the country: it's politics over people, extremes over rationality," Dean said.

After that, the two men launched into a fascinating exchange of their views on various topics. Dean said he was pro-life, while Earl talked about a woman's right to choose. Dean said he was pro-gun, while Earl talked about gun control. Earl wanted free government healthcare, while Dean didn't want the government to be part of his healthcare choices. Earl wanted fairer laws for immigrants, while Dean wanted more border security.

Suddenly, they both burst out laughing. They explained that they had been talking about these very topics for over a year.

"Santiago, every election is the same. People on each extreme push their agenda," Dean said.

"Sensible arguments seem to get thrown out the window, and politics becomes a game of who can be louder," Earl said.

"Or meaner," Dean added.

"Turn on the TV, and you'll see that most political ads attack the other candidate, instead of saying what their own candidate will do for the country. It's terrible," Earl said. "I hope someone can bring more decency to politics someday."

They both laughed out loud at that.

"That's why we both moved away from the extremes," Dean said. "The extremes are trying to take over the country. I hope your generation doesn't let them get away with that."

The extremes? Bringing decency back to politics? Throughout my entire life, I'd thought that American politicians were well-centered, honest, and admirable. The more I spoke to regular Americans though, the more my thoughts about American politics changed.

After sharing more stories and drinking another cup of coffee, it was time to say goodbye to my two new friends. In the following weeks, I saw how they would faithfully meet at that coffee shop every week to share their friendship over a cup of coffee. They were two people with opposite viewpoints, but they took the time to listen to each other, even if they disagreed in most matters.

On my walk home that day, I observed the beautiful homes in my neighborhood. It was fall now, and most of the trees had changed colors, making the landscape unique. Everything was clean, pristine, and appeared to be perfect. I thought about my conversation with Dean and Earl and wondered if more people could be like them. I had always thought of the United States as a perfect place. But the more I learned about it, the more I realized that it wasn't.

Chapter Thirty-Two
HALLOWEEN

October 28, 2000

My first Halloween in Iowa was marked by two specific events: my first experience with the American tradition of trick-or-treating and my first time entering and escaping from a corn maze.

Marcus and Jonathan both had younger brothers and sisters, and they were planning on taking their siblings out trick-or-treating on Halloween. They explained that this was a tradition where children dress up in costumes and walk from house to house asking for candy while saying "trick or treat" to homeowners. Upon hearing this threat, if homeowners don't give children a treat, the children may perform mischief on the property. This was all new to me, as it was not a Peruvian tradition until very recently. Growing up, my family had three different traditions during this time of the year: the baptism of *Guaguas*, All Saint's Day, and the day of *La Canción Criolla*.

In my hometown, the baptism of the *Guaguas*—a sweet bread shaped like a baby—is an interesting tradition each year around this time. It is somewhat similar to the ceremony of baptism in the Catholic Church. It consists of someone—generally a man—gifting a *guagua* to a friend, and that person must then organize a "baptism ceremony," choosing from among their friends who would be the "father," "mother," "godparents," and "priest." The celebration takes the form of a dinner, and sharing the "baptized" *guagua* strengthens the bond among the participating friends. According to my mother, it is done to celebrate the Day of the Dead, reminding us that new life is formed after another is gone. I have also read that in some parts of South America, people bake this bread to share with the living on the Day of the Dead, and then they take any extra bread to the cemetery to place on tombs. I like my maternal grandmother's interpretation of the tradition best of all: it is an excuse to get together with friends and family and eat some good food.

All Saint's Day is a celebration of all Christian saints, and it usually falls on November 1. It is a public holiday in Peru, and many spend this day remembering their deceased loved ones. In my family, we would go to church and then to the cemetery to place flowers on my grandparents' tombs.

La canción criolla is celebrated on October 31. It celebrates a type of traditional folkloric music from coastal areas of Peru. My family celebrated this day, even though Arequipa is located in the Andes. On November 1, after visiting the cemetery, we would go to a traditional restaurant to eat some traditional Peruvian food and listen to live *música criolla*.

Although it was different—or perhaps *because* it was different—Halloween in Iowa was an interesting and unique experience for me. Marcus, Jonathan, and I met at Jonathan's place and rallied the troops: seven children dressed up in different costumes. We walked around the neighborhood, knocking on doors, and meeting many of the neighbors. It was a mildly cold Iowa night, and many parents sat on their front porches drinking warm beverages. The whole ordeal took about two hours. The children were beyond excited to get candy. There was only one rule with our group: no one could eat their candy until we were done trick-or-treating. Marcus said this was because we didn't want to have overly excited children walking around town while hyped up on too much sugar. Marcus's and Jonathan's parents forced them to take their siblings out, so they were not excited about spending their night babysitting children. I, on the other hand, was almost as excited as the kids. I saw countless Spidermen, princesses, football players, Hulks, and Supermen; a few farmers and baseball players; and even a little Neo, the main character of *The Matrix*.

Once we got back to Jonathan's house, all the parents were sitting on the porch drinking hot chocolate. The children were finally allowed to eat their candy—though not before paying Marcus, Jonathan, and me a "candy commission" for taking them trick-or-treating. Marcus had them line up and give each of us two pieces of candy, which we then pooled and shared amongst ourselves. When Marcus initially told me about this commission, I responded by saying that I wouldn't take candy from the kids. However, when I saw just how much candy they had received, I didn't feel too guilty.

My other Halloween experience that year involved a lot of pumpkins, a corn maze, and a few clowns. I'm not a fan of clowns. In fact, I'm a bit scared of them. I don't know how my fear of clowns started; I just know that I find them incredibly unsettling.

Marcus had asked me if I wanted to visit a corn maze with him. Sarah, Jonathan, and Jennifer would meet us there. He told me not to wear fancy shoes.

"Boots okay?" I asked.

"Yes, so long as they're not fancy. We're going to do a lot of walking and with the recent rain, it may be muddy."

Marcus picked me up in the middle of the afternoon, and we headed to a farm about ten minutes east of Mount Vernon. When we arrived, Sarah, Jonathan, and Jennifer were already sitting on a picnic table outside the farm, waiting by the ticket booth. "What is this place?" I asked, amazed.

"It's my uncle's farm. He has a pumpkin patch and a pretty cool corn maze," Marcus replied. "Come on, my uncle knows we're coming."

He walked up to the ticket booth—which was just a table with a lady handing out tickets in exchange for money—and asked for his uncle, who came out a few minutes later. We said hello and followed him into a house. There, he handed us a few tickets and a couple of coupons. With these, we could enter the corn maze and get some souvenirs and a free cup of hot chocolate.

Once we had our tickets, Marcus and Sarah led the way. We walked to a field filled with hundreds of pumpkins. Our coupons allowed us to get one pumpkin each. I grabbed a medium-sized one and asked Jonathan, "What are we supposed to do with this?"

"You can carve them," he responded.

I had never carved a pumpkin before, so I didn't know what he meant. "Why?"

"It's for Halloween. You can put a candle in it, like that," he explained, pointing to a few carved pumpkins lined up in front of a couple of scarecrows.

I walked toward the carved pumpkins and examined them. The tops of the pumpkins had been cut off to form a lid, the inside flesh—including all the seeds—had been scooped out, a candle had been placed inside the pumpkin, and an image was carved in one side, exposing the hollow interior. After I examined those pumpkins with a great deal of curiosity, Marcus called me back over to help him take our group's pumpkins to his car. We placed all the pumpkins in a small wagon for transportation and then loaded them into the trunk of Marcus's car.

"Ready for the corn maze?" he asked as we walked back to the farm.

"Yeah, about that: what do we do in a 'corn maze'?" I had never been to a corn maze before, so I didn't know what to expect.

"Don't worry, my uncle's corn maze isn't too bad. You won't even get very lost. Just walk, though. Don't run."

Why would I need to run? I thought.

With that, we all grabbed some bottles of water, snacks, flashlights, and, since it had rained a lot over the past few days, some wooden hiking sticks and headed to the corn maze.

As we walked into the maze, I noticed a sign that read: "Welcome to the Haunted Maze." Wait, a haunted maze? "Marcus, what do they mean by 'haunted'?" I asked. I had been in haunted houses before, but never in a maze.

"It's like a haunted house, Santiago. You'll be fine," he replied, shrugging off my question.

At the entrance of the maze, a person wearing overalls and a sombrero explained some of the rules. He said it should take us between thirty and forty-five minutes to walk through the maze. He asked us to not touch any of the "monsters." Some of them were actual people, but some of them were machines. None of them were dangerous, though; they were just there to supply some good Halloween fun.

I'm not afraid of scary movies, but I don't do well in haunted houses. It's not that I'm scared of the monsters, skeletons, or bugs one may encounter in a haunted house; I just don't do well with the surprise factor. I was starting to get nervous about this "haunted" corn maze.

We walked in as a group, but quickly separated. Jonathan and Jennifer took the first left turn while Marcus, Sarah, and I took a right. As we walked through the maze, creepy music played over loudspeakers. Suddenly, a person wearing a zombie mask jumped out of the corn at the corner of the pathway up ahead. Sarah screamed, Marcus laughed, and my heartrate rose. The masked individual scampered away, so we kept walking.

As we made our way through the maze, we encountered more people dressed up like monsters, skeletons, and vampires. I was able to remain calm throughout all of this, until I confronted my worst nightmare: a clown with long orange hair, crooked teeth, dark-colored clothes, and a creepy laugh. That was it for me.

All of the talk about not running and not touching the individuals in the maze went completely out of the window. I pushed the terrifying clown and, although my knee still hurt a bit from my meniscus tear, I took off running. Marcus and Sarah desperately called for me to stop, but I was already hightailing it out of there. I could hear people asking me to stop running, but I didn't slow down. I couldn't. I turned right, left, and right again. I was lost, but I had to keep going. Then, I noticed that someone was following me. I didn't want to look around to see who it was, but when I did, my heartrate peaked, and I lost the ability to think clearly. The person following me and asking me to stop running was none other than the clown. I took off running again, this time even faster.

It took me about thirty minutes to find my way out of the corn maze. By the time I got to the exit, I was tired and sweating, but relieved that my nightmare had finally come to an end. However, there was one more issue I had to face: the area right outside the maze's exit was very muddy, and in my efforts to escape, I lost my balance, slipped, and fell. My jeans were now covered in mud.

With my heart still racing, and my body muddy and sweaty, I walked to the barn by the farm's entrance. Inside, I washed my face and tried to clean my muddy jeans and shoes as best I could. Back outside, I walked to a small concession stand and got my free cup of hot chocolate. Then I walked back to the corn maze and sat down on a bench to wait for my friends.

Sarah and Marcus emerged first. Then, a few minutes later, Jonathan and Jennifer did the same.

"Santiago, what happened to you?" Marcus asked when he saw me. "You took off after you saw that clown."

"I hate clowns."

"But man, running in the maze is dangerous."

"I know. I just can't do clowns."

"Alright, alright," Marcus said as they all started laughing. I couldn't believe I had just run like that, all because of a clown. I was a bit embarrassed, but relieved to know that it was all over. Or so I thought.

On our way out, Marcus's uncle came over to talk to us. He had heard about my experience and apologized about it. I told him that it was my fault and that I should be the one apologizing for running in the maze. Then, a hand touched my left shoulder, and someone asked, "Are you okay, man?" I turned to see who had spoken to me, and it was the *clown*!

I stood there, not saying a word, and turned pale.

"Are you alright?" he repeated.

"He's afraid of clowns," Marcus said.

The clown laughed and said, "Alright, then. I should leave before I cause any more trouble."

My friends just laughed at it all. After a while, I did, too, though I will never be able to forget that face... the face of that Iowa clown.

Chapter Thirty-Three
TOO CLOSE TO CALL

November 7, 2000

In the weeks leading up to the presidential election, I met with Professor Connor, a friend of the Petersons and a political science professor at the University of Iowa. He knew that I was interested in American politics and agreed to explain the election process to me. Kenneth drove me to the Java House, one of my favorite coffee shops in Iowa City, where I met with Professor Connor.

After we grabbed a cup of coffee and found a small table in the back of the coffee shop, he asked me about my exchange program and my political curiosity in general. I told him that I'd had a wonderful year thus far and that because of the different political crises I had experienced in Peru, I wanted to learn more about American politics. He seemed eager to share his knowledge with me and got right down to business: "Alright, Santiago, where do you want to start?"

"I don't understand why people talk about an 'Electoral College' when electing the next president. What's that? And why does it matter?"

"In this country, the people don't actually elect the president. At least not directly."

"What? Then who does?"

"The Electoral College." Professor Connor explained that the Founding Fathers had established the Electoral College as a sort of compromise between a vote in Congress and a popular vote of qualified citizens to determine the next president. The Founding Fathers had apparently been concerned that a demagogue—or a tyrant—could manipulate the masses to take power, so they decided that having qualified electors would ensure that only a qualified person would become president. He also explained that each state has a pre-determined number of Electoral College votes, all of which add up to 538 votes. A candidate needs at least 270 votes to win the presidential election.

"So what are the people actually voting for, then?" I asked, confused.

"They vote at the state level. Practically speaking, their vote decides how their state will vote in the Electoral College."

"Hold on, let me get this straight: if a state has ten Electoral College votes, and a candidate gets sixty percent of the popular vote in that state, then that candidate gets six Electoral College votes?" I asked.

"Not quite. Most states have a 'winner-take-all' rule for the Electoral College. This means that in those states, whichever candidate gets a majority of the popular vote gets all the Electoral College votes."

I paused for a moment, trying to understand this process. It didn't make much sense to me. "So if you vote for a Republican in a state with a Democrat majority, your vote essentially doesn't count, right?"

"Elaborate a bit more," he responded.

"Let's say you vote for a Republican, but the majority of your state votes for a Democrat. In that case, all of your state's Electoral College votes go to the Democratic candidate," I said.

"That's right—for the most part. There are a couple of states that don't follow the 'winner-take-all' rule."

"It seems like an unfair rule. How is that democratic?" I asked.

"Many argue that it's not. I think it makes states with smaller populations matter a lot more than they otherwise would," he said.

"How so?"

"One argument is that if we don't use the Electoral College system and move to a strict popular-vote election, the president would be decided by the big cities, not the states."

"But what about the people? They're voting for the president of the United States, not for the governor of their state," I argued.

"That's one of the arguments against the Electoral College."

We discussed more of the arguments for and against the Electoral College system, and Professor Connor explained how a popular vote would have its own set of issues. Then he said something that completely shocked me: "Another problem we have is low turnout for voting."

"Low turnout? How much is the fine for not voting?" I asked, taken aback. By law, all Peruvian citizens are required to vote in all presidential, congressional, and local elections, and there is a fine—ranging from twenty to eighty *soles* depending on how wealthy or poor the local jurisdiction is— for not doing so.

"Santiago, voting isn't mandatory in the United States."

"You're kidding."

"No. If you don't want to vote, you don't have to. And often, many people can't vote."

"Why?"

"Presidential and midterm elections are held in November, and in many places like Iowa, the weather can be bad. Many don't vote because they can't get to their polling station due to snow or ice. Others don't vote because they can't get away from work or duties at home. And some simply forget."

I told him that, in Peru, elections are on a Sunday, when most people don't work, and even for those who have to work on a Sunday, public entities and businesses are required to give workers a break, so they can exercise their right to vote.

"Elections are held on a Tuesday in this country."

"On a Tuesday? That would prevent a lot of people from voting. Who is the genius who decided to schedule elections on a Tuesday?" I asked. The more I learned, the more this system seemed to be poorly thought out.

"It goes back to the 1800s, when many people were farmers and lived far away from their polling place. Sundays were for church, and Wednesdays were market days. Tuesdays were just the most convenient days."

"But we're not in the 1800s anymore. Times have changed. Why don't they change the date?" I asked.

"I'm not sure. I guess we're just used to it," he responded.

"And why November?"

"Again, it was because of the farmers in the 1800s. Spring and summer were their busy times, and winter was simply too harsh for them to get to polling places. Late fall, after harvest was over, was the best time of the year for voting."

"But you just said that it snows in November sometimes."

"It's not a perfect system," Professor Connor said sagely.

We discussed the American political system for a while longer, addressing the advantages and disadvantages of the two-party system. We also talked about the coming election in November. Professor Connor was a Democrat, and he thought Al Gore would be the winner. I wasn't sure about that. Although I thought that Gore would win because a Gore administration would likely continue the policies of the Clinton administration and most people seemed to want that, Bush seemed a lot more convincing—and definitely more charming—than Gore during the presidential debates.

In the following weeks, I gained a greater appreciation for the American political system. It was a complex, somewhat confusing, and always evolving system that appeared to be working well thus far.

On Election Day, I was glued to the television. Initially, it seemed that Professor Connor was right, and that Al Gore would become the next president of the United States. But then, it looked like George W. Bush would win. By the time I finally went to bed, it was deemed "too close to call."

During my year in the United States I learned a lot about American politics—probably more than most teenagers do when they travel to a different country. Of course, I was interested in politics, just like I was interested in soccer, track, and music. If I'd had the same interest in acting or mathematics, I'd have joined the theater or the math clubs, and this book would have more chapters about those subjects. That's the beauty of the experience: no two exchange students are the same, because we all have different backgrounds and unique personal interests. I felt extremely lucky to get to live in the United States during an election year, as it was a perfect opportunity to learn more about the American political system.

In the end, Al Gore did win. He won the popular vote. George W. Bush, however, won the presidential election. He won the Electoral College vote. What a mess.

Chapter Thirty-Four
TAKING THE TEST

November 18, 2000

"So Santiago, what are you planning on doing after this year is over?" Kenneth asked me one day.

"I'm going back to Peru," I responded, not knowing what he meant. My exchange program through the Rotary Club was for a single year, and I had planned to attend college in Peru after my time in Iowa. Besides, my student visa was only for a year, so I had to go back. "Why do you ask?"

"Have you ever thought about going to college in the United States?"

I honestly hadn't. My goal had been to learn as much as I could during my year in Iowa, grow as a person, learn a new language, and then leave. I had no interest in coming back. "No, I haven't. I have plans to go to college in Peru," I responded.

"I'll tell you what: let's meet my friend Allen at Cornell College this weekend." Allen worked in the admissions department at Cornell, a small private college in Mount Vernon. "He can show you around the school. No pressure, but I think you should at least take a tour and see what college is like in the United States," he said.

I had visited the University of Iowa in Iowa City and Drake University in Des Moines with some friends before, but not as part of a formal visit. I didn't want to tour schools while I was in Iowa, mostly because I didn't want to create any unrealistic expectations for myself. After I had learned that many of my high school friends at Mount Vernon were planning to attend college, I had glanced at the cost of going to school in the United States, and realized that the prospect of attending an American college was out of my reach, financially. I didn't want to say no to Kenneth though, as he was always so nice to me. "Sure, let's do it," I said.

He made a couple of phone calls and scheduled the visit. Kenneth and I would visit the school on Saturday, a current student would show us around the campus, we would have lunch in the cafeteria, and then we'd have a meeting with Allen and another member of the admissions team.

The day of my tour, we met Allen outside the admissions office. Although it was a cold Saturday morning, I was comfortable, as I had properly "winterized." Allen introduced me to Emily, a third-year student who would be our tour guide. After some small talk, Kenneth, Emily, and I went on our way.

Emily was charming, which is exactly what you'd expect from a college tour guide. She showed us the administrative buildings, the dorms, and some classrooms. The school was definitely a beautiful place. She also asked me about my interests: "Are there any sports that might interest you?"

"Yes, I played soccer in high school and ran track in Peru."

"Long distance?"

"No, I'm a sprinter," I said. Most people didn't see me as a sprinter due to my thin frame.

"Cool. Want to check out the athletic fields?" she asked.

I nodded, and Emily took us over to the soccer fields. I was impressed with their quality. Even though they seemed to be a bit rough due to the harsh weather conditions, they were flat and, most importantly, full of grass. Many of the fields I had played on in Peru contained more dirt and rocks than grass.

Next, she led us over to the track. She explained that they were remodeling it, but even as it was, it was in infinitely better shape than the one I had practiced and competed on in Arequipa. How could it be that a small private college in a town of about four thousand people had a better track and field stadium than Arequipa, a city of over one million people? Seeing me admire it, Emily asked with a smile, "Do you like it? Perhaps you'll run on it someday."

"Perhaps," I answered noncommittally, trying to keep the wistfulness out of my voice. Although the campus had already deeply impressed me, and my tour guide was doing a great job, I didn't want to set up any unrealistic expectations. My plan was to attend school in Peru, and I had no intention of changing it.

We walked around campus for another hour before heading back to the admissions office to meet Allen. "How was the tour?" he asked when we entered.

"Pretty good. A bit cold, though," I quipped.

"Hopefully you can get used to it," he said as we sat down around a table. I smiled politely, but I was not convinced.

Allen gave us a couple of folders with information about the school. I quickly reviewed them, and among all the beautiful pictures of the campus, I found a page that listed the tuition and fees. At that moment, my suspicions were confirmed. The total cost of tuition, room, and board for one year was over twenty-five thousand dollars. That was an impossible sum for my family. For comparison, at the time, it cost about thirty thousand dollars to purchase a nice two-bedroom condo in an exclusive area of my hometown. I felt that my entire visit had been a waste of time. While Allen talked about the application process, possible scholarships, and requirements for international students, all I could think about was the cost.

When our meeting was over, we thanked Allen for his time and walked to Kenneth's car. "Thoughts?" Kenneth asked as we climbed into the car and turned on the blessed heater.

"It's expensive," I said.

"I know. College is expensive. You should take that English test Allen told you about anyway."

"Which test?" After I'd noticed the cost of tuition and other fees, I'd stopped paying attention.

"Let me see." He grabbed one of the folders and rifled through it. "Here it is: the Test of English as a Foreign Language, or TOEFL. It's one of the requirements for international students."

"Why bother? I can't afford to go to school here. Besides, I'm going to attend college in Peru."

"Just take it. There's enough time for you to schedule a test before you leave," he said. "You never know what will happen in the future, and having a good TOEFL score may help."

I was annoyed. I wasn't planning on going to school in the United States, so why would I take that test? It made no sense, but for some reason, I agreed. When we got home, we got online and scheduled a test, which would be in a couple of weeks.

I didn't do much to prepare for it, and about two weeks later, Kenneth took me to Iowa City to take the TOEFL. I thought I did reasonably well, and my scores arrived a couple of weeks later. My score was, in fact, excellent.

"What do I do with this now?" I asked Kenneth after I opened the envelope with my score.

"Save it. You never know what the future holds, Santiago. You may need it someday."

"I'm not so sure about that," I said. "At least I got it before I have to fly back home."

Chapter Thirty-Five
FELIZ NAVIDAD

December 25, 2000

I did not spend Christmas in Iowa. Instead, my host family took a trip to Naperville, a wealthy suburb south of Chicago, to visit Ellen, Kenneth's mother. We had already visited Naperville earlier that fall, so Ellen was a familiar face. She is a kind, highly educated, and independent woman. She had graduated from Illinois State University with a science degree at a time when women rarely studied science. We've kept in touch over the years, and I consider her one of my greatest mentors. At the time, she lived by herself in a small, but charming, home in a beautiful area of Naperville.

We left Mount Vernon on a frigid Friday afternoon, and the trip to Naperville took about four hours. During that time, Linda took a long nap in the backseat, while Kenneth and I talked about our different Christmas traditions. This was my first Christmas in the United States, and I wanted to get a glimpse of what I was getting myself into.

Kenneth explained that every family is different, but there is a pattern that many families in the Midwest follow: getting together on Christmas Eve for dinner, a church ceremony or service for the religious bunch, and opening presents on Christmas morning.

"So people don't wait until midnight on Christmas Eve to celebrate together?" I asked, surprised.

"No. I've actually never heard of such a thing. What do you mean by 'waiting until midnight'?"

"In Peru, my family gets together on Christmas Eve, and we all stay up until midnight to celebrate the birth of Jesus," I said. "That's when we open presents."

"That doesn't happen here. In fact, many kids go to bed as soon as they can on Christmas Eve, so that Christmas Day comes faster," he said.

When I was growing up in Peru, we would attend Christmas Eve mass around six p.m., and then my extended family would gather at my paternal grandmother's home or my maternal grandmother's home, depending on the year, for dinner. We all had dinner together, and it was rather chaotic. Many members of my family tend to talk rather loudly and over each other, so having dinner with about fifteen people was a loud event. The kids drank *chicha morada*—a delicious purple-colored juice made with the chilled water from boiled purple corn with added lime juice, sugar, and chunks of apples or pineapples. It tastes a bit like Kool-Aid. The adults drank wine or another alcoholic beverage. The food was always a delicious treat. Every family who attended dinner brought a dish—as generally seen at an Iowa potluck—and the dining table was filled with delicious pasta salads, rice, sweet potatoes, tamales, and other dishes, all arranged around a delicious baked turkey. While Americans eat turkey during Thanksgiving, most Peruvians eat it at Christmas. That poor bird just can't catch a break.

After dinner, the adults would gather in the living room or on my grandmother's patio to chat while the kids went outside to play on the street. All the children on the block would come out, and we had wonderful times together. We played hide and seek, rode our skateboards, or got together under a tree to tell scary stories. I loved it. At the time, that small street didn't have to worry about crime or vandalism. Today, it has security gates on each end of it.

Fifteen or twenty minutes before midnight, the parents would call their children inside to clean up—and calm down. By now, all the presents were placed next to the nativity scene. Although Santa Claus—or Papá Noel, as Peruvians call him—has become part of the Peruvian tradition in recent years, most families still continue the tradition in which baby Jesus is the one bringing presents for all.

At midnight, we would all stand in front of the nativity scene, and my grandmother would pick up the small piece of cloth that had covered baby Jesus for days, making it official: Jesus is born.

About eighty-five percent of Peruvians are Catholic, including my family, so most of the Christmas traditions in Peru are Christian ones. However, presents are also a big part of Christmas. After my grandmother uncovered baby Jesus and led a prayer, we all hugged and exchanged gifts.

While all of this was happening inside at midnight, many Peruvians would light fireworks outside. Although setting off fireworks without a license is illegal in Peru, the authorities turn a blind eye to it at Christmas, and thousands of families light fireworks all over the city. The kids, of course, were the ones most excited with all the commotion.

After we opened our presents, we would play outside with our friends—and our new toys—for a couple of hours until our parents called us back to go home. Christmas night is usually a long night.

On Christmas morning, my family would have hot chocolate with a piece of *panetón*, or *panettone*, a kind of Italian sweet bread commonly consumed in many South American countries. We then visited the "other" grandmother, had leftovers for lunch, and opened more presents. Although no family's tradition is the same, I'd bet that a good number of Peruvian families follow a similar pattern.

When we arrived in Naperville, Ellen welcomed us with a warm hug. Ellen's home was decorated like many of the homes in her neighborhood: with Christmas lights around the windows and on the tree at the front yard, a beautiful wreath hanging on the front door, and some elegant Christmas decorations on the windows. Inside, a small nativity scene brightened one corner of the living room, a lovely red and green centerpiece decorated the dining room table, and small Santa figurines seemed to pop up on every surface.

When I entered the living room, I found the biggest surprise of the day: a tall, majestic, and very real Christmas tree stood in one corner of the room. I had never seen a real Christmas tree before. All of the Christmas trees we ever had back home were plastic ones. Even the Petersons—who usually got a real tree every Christmas—had put up an artificial tree that year. Its beauty perplexed me. I'm not exaggerating when I say that I stood in front of it in awe for several minutes.

Ellen walked me up the stairs to the second floor and showed me to "my room." Right at the top of the stairs was a carpeted area with a big sofa, a computer desk in one corner, and a small bookshelf next to it.

"Santiago, you can put your bags there," she said, pointing to the computer desk. "Let's pull out your bed."

I thought she meant that we would get an air mattress or a small bed from another room. Instead, she pointed at the sofa and asked me to pull one of the side levers. To my surprise, an actual bed folded out of that spacious sofa. I had never seen such a thing before; in Peru, my family had a regular sofa, not one with "transformer" capabilities.

Ellen helped me make my bed, and then we headed downstairs to the kitchen, where Kenneth and Linda were waiting for us. While Ellen and I had been setting up my bed, the Petersons had prepared dinner for us: chicken salad sandwiches for all. During dinner, Ellen told us the plan for the weekend: we would go to Chicago on Saturday, visit family members on Christmas Eve, spend Christmas Day at Ellen's house, and then drive back to Iowa on Tuesday.

As promised, on Saturday afternoon, Kenneth drove the four of us to the Amtrak train station in Naperville so we could jump on a train to Chicago. He wanted to avoid driving to the city during Christmas weekend, which could be a nightmare due to the heavy holiday traffic. The ride to Chicago was smooth. As we approached the city, I was able to see the iconic Willis Tower—although I still refer to it as the Sears Tower, its former name—the tallest building in the Chicago skyline.

We arrived in Chicago around two in the afternoon. The train dropped us off at Union Station, an iconic structure in the city. Its marble floors, brass lamps, and massive columns made it a beautiful sight to behold. It was busy, though. Not only is it one of the busiest train terminals in the United

States, but the holiday season also made it a bit overwhelming.

As we walked out of the station, the cold temperature slapped me in the face. I knew it would be a cold day in the city, and I had properly winterized, but I had not accounted for the wind. As we walked toward Millennium Park, the wind seemed to become even stronger, and it was not kind to my face. The Petersons were aware of my cold allergy, and we made several stops at different stores to warm up as we approached Michigan Avenue.

One thing that stood out to me during our stops was that most stores had "Happy Holidays" signs. I had grown up in a country that only celebrated Christmas, so it took me some time—and a great deal of exposure and cultural curiosity—to understand the meaning behind those two words. It wasn't until the following Christmas that I learned that other people celebrate different mid-winter holidays than I did, and that "Merry Christmas" was not as universal as I had once thought.

When we finally made it to Michigan Avenue, we stopped at a coffee shop to get something warm to drink. I welcomed this stop, as my face had started to hurt a bit due to the cold. I ordered some hot chocolate, and we sat down at one of the tables.

"Santiago, what do you think so far? Do you like Chicago during Christmas?" Kenneth asked.

"It's wonderful," I said. The city lights and decorations made it seem so festive. In Peru, my hometown was decorated during Christmas, but not as extensively as Chicago. After a short pause, I added, "It's different."

The Christmas season in Peru *is* very different. For starters, in December, it's summer in the Southern Hemisphere, so people don't walk around wearing winter clothes. There's no snow on the ground. In 2000, the Chicago area had a record amount of snow in December, and although it did not snow during that Christmas weekend, there was plenty of snow on the ground. It was truly a white Christmas, something I had never experienced before. The main difference to me, however, was that the holiday season in the United States seemed to be more about buying things for others than anything else. Buying presents was—and still is—a big part of Christmas for my Peruvian family, but the purpose of the season for us was to celebrate the birth of Jesus, not to find the latest toy. Most of the Peruvian television ads during this season were about families getting together, not about the latest and greatest Christmas sales. Due to globalization and because Peruvian society has become Americanized in many ways, there is now more of an emphasis on buying Christmas presents; however, the religious aspect of the season is still very much alive and well. During that holiday season in the United States, since I noticed a strong emphasis on buying presents for others everywhere, I bought a few presents for my host family with the little money I had.

We walked around Michigan Avenue for a couple of hours. I bought a winter facemask at one of the stores we visited so I could better tolerate the cold temperatures. We saw a giant Christmas tree, and my family took a picture of me in front of it. We walked to Navy Pier and took more pictures with all the Christmas lights and decorations. Sunset in Chicago during that time of the year is around five p.m., and the temperature falls quickly after the sun leaves for the day, so we didn't stay out for too long after that. Ellen made a comment about her feet starting to hurt, so we made our way back to the train station and went home.

The following two days were a bit of a blur. We visited Ellen's relatives on Christmas Eve and had dinner with them. There was a lot of food, and all of the people I met were very nice. On Christmas Day, we exchanged gifts at Ellen's home and spent the day watching Christmas movies, taking naps, and telling family stories. I did stay up until midnight on Christmas Eve and called my Peruvian family to wish them all a "*Feliz Navidad*."

Surprisingly, I wasn't sad about spending Christmas away from my family. I was excited to experience Christmas in a different country, with different traditions. At the time, I didn't know that I would not spend Christmas with them again for over ten years.

We left for Iowa the day after Christmas. That trip back is also a blur to me. Kenneth and I talked more about the history of Chicago. It had already become my favorite city in the United States, and about twenty years later, it still is. Not only do I love its classy and majestic downtown scene, the beautiful lake surrounded by carefully manicured parks, its unique skyline with breathtaking views, and all the life and culture it holds, but I also love it because I spent my first American *Navidad* in one of its suburbs.

Chapter Thirty-Six
IOWA

January 13, 2001

On my last day in Iowa, I was in the basement bathroom, trying to fix my hair, which had grown out of control, when I heard the phone ringing. "Santiago, phone for you! It's Carrie," Linda shouted from the kitchen.

I ran to the phone and noticed that Kenneth was holding one of my bags. "What are you taking back to Peru, rocks?" he asked. I had packed as much as possible in one of my bags, while the other bag was half-empty. Poor planning on my part. Still, I'd deal with it later.

"Hi, Carrie. How are you?" I said when I picked up the phone.

"Hey! I'm doing pretty well. How are you? Ready for your trip back?" she asked cheerfully.

"Not really. I may have to readjust my bags. I think one of them is too heavy."

She laughed. "That's not what I meant. Are you ready to go home, to see your family?"

"I think so," I said. Truthfully, I wasn't sure if I *was* ready to go home. I wanted to see my Peruvian family and friends and share all my experiences with them, but I also wished I could stay in Iowa a little longer. The Novaks and the

Petersons had been wonderful to me. Mount Vernon had been a great place to live, and Iowa had found its way into my heart.

"I'm sure you are, Santiago. It'll be good to see your family," Carrie said. I could tell she was holding back tears. "We'll see you at the airport."

"See you soon," I responded before hanging up.

I went back down to the basement. Kenneth was still eyeing my bags warily. "Are you sure you'll be able to take this bag? It feels a bit too heavy to me," Kenneth said with a classic smirk on his face.

"You're right: I should rearrange my clothes. Want to do it for me?" I teased. He knew I was joking.

"Nope. It's all you, Santiago," he said, laughing, as he walked up to the kitchen.

I rearranged my belongings as quickly as I could. I didn't have much of a system and just moved clothes, shoes, and souvenirs from one bag to the other. The goal was to even out their weight. After a few minutes, I deemed them ready. I just hoped that the customs officials in Lima wouldn't make me open them, as they were rather disorganized. At the time, the Lima International Airport had a system whereby passengers' bags were randomly selected for inspection.

"Kenneth, I'm ready now," I called up the stairs. "Could you give me a hand?"

"Sure, after lunch. Come on up. It's ready."

Linda had made her specialty: grilled cheese sandwiches. By the time I got up there, Kenneth was already complimenting her on her cooking. I was going to miss them. They had been so wonderful to me, and it was great to be around a couple that was so happy even after so many years together. Kenneth and I exchanged jokes as usual, though Linda was a bit quiet. She seemed anxious.

After lunch, Kenneth helped me load my bags into their SUV. Linda placed a card for me in my carry-on bag and asked me not to open it until I arrived in Lima. It was cold out, so I grabbed my winter coat and bundled up before saying goodbye to Max. He affectionately licked my hand one last time.

Kenneth drove to the Cedar Rapids airport, while Linda took the front passenger seat. She was in charge of the radio. Our drive to the airport was a quiet one, and we needed some good background music. As we drove to the airport, I thought about my year in Mount Vernon. I wondered why I had ended up in Iowa, of all places. For most people in the United States, Iowa was just another state in the Midwest, some farmland in "flyover country." But for me, Iowa wasn't just where I had lived for a year. Iowa was family, friends, and memories. Iowa was home.

What made this place so special for me? Easy: its people.

Iowa isn't the place to find big-city living. Des Moines is a growing city, but it isn't Chicago, New York, or even Kansas City. And I'm not sure it actually wants to be like those places. Iowa isn't the place to see thousands of strangers from all over the world wandering around aimlessly and looking at a thousand lights. In fact, I could probably count all the billboards in Mount Vernon with my two hands.

Yet Iowa was the place where I had learned English. Although it was the place where I had been bullied and discriminated against for the first time in my life because I was different, it was also the place where I learned that people who truly care about you will protect you. My year in

Mount Vernon was unforgettable because of its people—kind, hardworking, humble, good-hearted people. I know this may be a generalization, but that's the image I still have of this beautiful and, yes, rather flat state.

At the airport, the Petersons and the Novak clan bade me goodbye. I hugged each one of them in turn. After I got my boarding pass, I approached my gate and waved to them one last time. Saying goodbye was harder than I'd thought it would be.

Once I got settled in my seat on the plane, I reached into my carry-on bag and pulled out the card Linda had placed there. I knew she didn't want me to open it until I arrived in Lima, but I couldn't wait. I opened it and found that the front featured a picture of a cornfield with the words "Life is…" in the middle of it. Inside, a silhouette of the state of Iowa was surrounded an anthropomorphic corncob that said, "…better in a cornfield." Although I knew Iowa was much more than cornfields, I smiled. Opposite the talking corncob, Linda had written a personal message, saying that she and Kenneth would miss me and wished me the best for my future. She also wrote, "I hope you're taking a piece of Iowa with you, in your heart, because you will always be remembered here. Iowa will always be your home."

I closed my eyes and thought back over my year in Mount Vernon. I remembered the moment I threw rocks in the Novaks' pond and thought about making ripples in what I called the "Iowa pond." I realized now that not only had I made some big ripples, but my life had impacted other people's lives in a permanent manner. I wondered if I would ever go back and if I would ever see any of those people again.

Chapter Thirty-Seven
WELCOME HOME

January 14, 2001

I arrived in Lima a few minutes after sunrise. Once the airplane stopped at the gate—or, more accurately, just prior to the plane coming to a full stop at the gate—most people started unbuckling their seatbelts and standing up. This didn't make sense to me, as we hadn't even stopped yet. I didn't stand up. In fact, I didn't even move. The lady sitting next to me asked me whether I was going to stand.

"Why would I do that?" I asked. "The plane hasn't even stopped yet." We were sitting in the back of the plane, and unless there was an emergency, we needed to wait for everyone else to exit the plane before we could move. Unless that lady could fly over people, she was stuck back there.

She gave me a rude look and stood up by her seat, regardless. After a rather long wait, people in front of us started to move. I stood up and began filing out after them. "Finally," she muttered. I didn't respond. I was too exhausted. I simply walked out of the plane and headed to customs and immigration.

As I approached customs, I noticed that a long line had formed. Two planes from the United States had arrived in the past thirty minutes, each plane with more than a hundred passengers.

There were four immigration officials working at the time. Three of them were checking passports for "the masses," while the fourth was responsible for the VIP line. While the immigration lines for us common folks were backed up, the VIP line was empty. After I noticed this inefficient way to handle traffic, I approached one of the airport employees. "The VIP line is empty. Why don't you open it to the general public?" I asked.

"Sir, we can't. It's for VIPs," she answered simply.

"What do I need to do to be a VIP?"

"Are you a diplomat?" she asked.

"No."

"Are you or one of your relatives a public official?"

"No, not that I know of."

"Then please join that line," she said, pointing at one of the long lines. I didn't want to argue with her, as she was simply doing her job, but I was frustrated with the process. I couldn't stop looking at the VIP immigration official sitting at her desk doing nothing and with no one to help, while her three colleagues had to check the passports of more than two hundred people.

I finally made it to the commoners' immigration officer. He was courteous and asked me a few questions about my trip and my final destination.

"Can I ask you a question?" I asked. "That VIP line has been empty since we arrived. Why don't you guys open it up to everyone?"

"That's beyond me, sir. I didn't make that call," he answered politely. With that, he checked my passport, stamped it, and put some papers inside it. I took another look at the VIP immigration officer. There still wasn't a soul by her desk.

"Thank you," I said. "Maybe you can ask your manager to open that line."

He raised his eyebrows and smirked at me. "I'll see what I can do, sir. Welcome home." I smiled and walked away. My first interaction with a Peruvian in Peru in almost a year was to point out an inefficiency at the airport. It was a reminder that Peru had a lot of work to do to catch up with more advanced and efficient countries.

As I walked to the baggage-claim area, I began to notice things I hadn't noticed before. People appeared to be smaller, smells seemed to be stronger, and the airport was much louder than I remembered it being. Although things were familiar, everything seemed new to me. Peru was my home country, but I felt that something had changed, although I couldn't pinpoint what yet. *What's changed? Is it me?* I thought.

I picked up my bag, and as I approached the exit, I noticed my uncle Gonzalo waving at me. Gonzalo, a banker, was married to my aunt Ana. "Santiago! Over here," he yelled. I hurried over and gave him a hug, and he took one of my bags. When we got to his car, he gave me a mint. Apparently, my breath revealed that I had been on a plane for over ten hours and hadn't had a chance to brush my teeth. I was slightly embarrassed.

"Hungry?" he said.

"Starving," I responded with feeling.

He took me out for breakfast at a restaurant in Miraflores. Although I was rather tired, our trip to the restaurant quickly woke me up. Unlike my aunt Ana, Gonzalo was an experienced driver and knew his way around Lima. He was an aggressive driver, too. I quickly noticed that after living in Iowa for about a year, it was going to take me some time to get used to Peruvian traffic again.

Back at Ana and Gonzalo's condo, I took a shower and turned on the television. Gonzalo had to go to work, so he couldn't stay too long. My aunt and cousin were already gone for the day. They were at their local country club, where my four-year-old cousin was taking swimming lessons. It was summer back in Peru, so it was the perfect time for it. As I searched for the sports channels, I smiled. I suddenly realized that it no longer mattered whether a channel was in Spanish or English. I understood both. It didn't matter whether I watched CNN in English or CNN *en Español*. My world was no longer limited to the Spanish-speaking world.

I watched TV until my aunt Ana and little cousin Luciana came home. I was excited to see them and had brought a small stuffed animal for Luciana from the United States. Seeing it, she gave me a big hug. She loved it.

Unfortunately, I couldn't spend much time with them. I had to leave for Arequipa that afternoon. Flying was expensive, so I had to take a bus. A fourteen-hour trip awaited me. Ana took me to the bus station, and a few hours later, I was on my way home.

I don't remember much about that bus trip. It's mostly a blur. I do remember, however, seeing my parents at the bus terminal when I arrived in Arequipa. I noticed the big smile on my mother's face when she saw me coming down the bus steps. I didn't get the same reaction from my father, though. He seemed concerned, almost sad.

"Santiago!" my mother exclaimed, giving me a big hug and a kiss on the cheek. She had tears in her eyes. My father also gave me a hug and a half smile. I could tell something was wrong. "Santiago, please ride back with your father," my mother said. Although my parents had separated two years earlier and their divorce was now final, they were still bitter and angry with each other.

"Okay, I'll see you at home," I agreed.

My dad took one of my bags, I grabbed the other, and we walked to the parking lot. I looked around for his car, a 1999 Nissan Sentra, but he walked toward a clunker instead. I was confused and wondered what had happened to his Nissan. Had he gotten into an accident recently? His face didn't convey his usual confidence. In fact, he seemed concerned, like a guy who wants to tell you that something is wrong, but doesn't have the guts to actually do so.

We climbed into the vehicle. It was dirty, and it showed its age. The last time I had seen my father, he wore a suit and drove a new car. Now, he was wearing an old pair of jeans that he'd had for decades and drove an old vehicle.

My father and I hadn't spoken much during my year in the United States. We were never "buddies," like some fathers and sons. Although he made sure we went to good schools and always had good food on the table, he struggled to display his emotions. On that day, however, it was apparent that something was wrong. *What happened?* I thought.

"How was your trip?" he asked casually.

"Good, Dad. I learned a lot."

"You're a lot bigger. It looks like you worked out," he said. After I hurt my knee playing football, I decided to hit the gym almost every day, and I'd gained a few pounds of muscle as a result.

"I did, but just in the last few months."

"That's good," he trailed off into silence. This whole time, he had avoided making eye contact.

"What's wrong?" I finally asked. We were stuck in the car together, so he couldn't escape my question.

He coughed, pressed his lips together, and finally responded, "I lost my job a few weeks ago. They took the company car. The market is tight, and I haven't been able to find a new one yet." Tears started to roll down his cheeks.

My father worked in the medical field. He was a pharmaceutical sales representative, a position that, at the time, did not require a college degree. He was a hard worker, and I could recall many nights when he had to study a new drug or a new market, and he stayed up late in his office, studying. Had he told me about losing his job before my trip to the United States, I would have panicked. I wouldn't have known what to say or do. However, my year in Iowa helped me realize that when bad things occur, the faster one can accept them, the faster one can move on and work to find solutions.

With that in mind, I looked my father in the eyes, leaned over across the console to give him a hug, and said, "I'm sorry. How are you doing?"

"I'm okay, but it's been hard," he said. I noticed his baggy eyes and thin arms. It was clear that he hadn't been sleeping well and had been losing weight.

"How are you health-wise? Is there anything that would prevent you from getting a new job?"

"No, not really," he said with a puzzled look.

"Then don't worry about it. You're healthy and capable. Sooner or later, you'll find a job. Worrying about it won't help anything," I said simply. I tried to evoke the same confidence that Kenneth displayed when giving me advice back in Iowa.

"Thank you," he said. He seemed surprised that I had spoken to him in such positive manner.

We settled back into a comfortable silence after that. Then, a thought struck me. "You know what? Let's go to Grandma's place so I can say hi to her. Mom will understand if we're a bit late," I suggested. My father's mother lived close to the bus terminal, so I figured it would be a good idea to stop by her house for a few minutes. Plus, this would give me a few more minutes with my father.

I ended up spending a couple of hours at my grandma's house. Her home was modest and in an unassuming neighborhood. I've always said that I have a "humble" grandmother and a "preppy" one. Both of them are sweet and wonderful, but they come from different backgrounds.

My father's mother is a retired teacher. When she was younger, she taught at a modest school. She didn't care much about money or possessions. All she cared about was that her family had food on the table and a roof over their heads and that they were hardworking people. She succeeded in all of this. She taught me to be humble, no matter how successful I would become.

In contrast, my mother's mother grew up in a family without financial struggles. Later, after she married my grandfather, they continued to do well. She wasn't rich by any means, but they were a comfortable middle-class family. She taught me that it was okay to be ambitious and want better things for your family.

On our way to my mother's home, my father and I talked about my trip and about my plans for the coming year. I told him that I wanted to go to the public university in Arequipa. It had already accepted me before my year in the United States, so it seemed like a logical choice. My father was happy about my decision. This university had a good reputation, and since it was a public university, it was basically free.

When he dropped me off, I said, "Thanks for the ride, Dad. I'll call you later this week."

By the time he dropped me off at home that day, my father seemed to have a different attitude entirely. In the end, it did take him a few months to find a new job, but he did eventually find one. A few years later, he thanked me for my words of encouragement that day. Given that he was a man of very few words himself, saying thank you was a lot for him.

"Sounds good. It's good to see you again," he said warmly. I smiled, grabbed my bags, and walked to the front door of my house.

I knocked, but no one opened it. Apparently, my mother had gone to the store to buy some groceries and had taken Jacinta, our maid, with her. They didn't return for another hour. My dad had already left, so all I could do was sit down by the front door with my bags and wait.

"Welcome home, Santiago," I whispered.

Chapter Thirty-Eight
THE BUBBLE BURST AGAIN

April 15, 2001

Back in Peru, there was an adjustment period. After I got over the initial excitement of seeing my family and friends again, I realized that life at home wasn't the same as it had been before my time in the United States.

In 2001, Peru was going through an unprecedented period of political uncertainty. During the fourth quarter of 2000, a corruption scandal involving Vladimiro Montesinos—the head of the national intelligence agency at the time—broke out. President Fujimori was left with no other choice than to call for new elections. The scandal involved several political figures—many of whom are, unfortunately, still part of Peruvian politics today—and had exploded into full force in September 2000 when a Peruvian television station showed a video of Montesinos bribing an opposition leader. Many more videos surfaced after that, and Fujimori's government collapsed. In November 2000, Fujimori took a trip to Brunei to attend an international forum and resigned from the presidency via fax. After that, Valentin Paniagua was elected by the Peruvian Congress as an interim president. He served until July 28, 2001, when Alejandro Toledo, another politician accused of corruption, took office.

In Peru, as in many parts of the world, many politicians start their political careers with good intentions, but with time, most of them end up taking the wrong path. I say "most" because I have to assume that there are a few who are honest and do things properly. But to me—and to most Peruvians—they are the exception, not the norm. With that intense distrust in Peruvian authorities in mind, I started school at a public university in Arequipa.

Unlike the United States, where students take standardized tests administered by private companies and send their scores to the schools of their choice as part of the admissions process, in Peru, most schools have their own standardized test. This means that if you wanted to apply to a specific school, you had to take their test. If you wanted to apply to five schools, you had to take five different tests. In addition, in the United States, students are also evaluated on their grade point average, extracurricular activities, and an essay. The most competitive schools even have an interview process. In Peru, admissions are based on how well a student does on the university's standardized test compared to others. That's it. Each school has a finite number of spots, so if your scores are not high enough to clinch a spot, the school won't admit you.

Fortunately, I had received a high score on my university entrance exam and was admitted. I say "fortunately" because, in Peru, the cost to attend most public universities is pretty low. I had to pay registration and other miscellaneous fees, and I had to buy my books, but I wasn't required to purchase the books at my school or at a specific bookstore. In fact, I could find pirated versions of books just around the corner from the school. I'm not proud of that, but it's just part of the culture.

In the United States, most college students don't live at home; they live in dorms on campus. It's part of the American college experience. In Peru, I lived at home like most students. I had free room and board, and since the school was close to my house, I could walk to it. In other words, I was getting a free education, cheap books, free housing, and I didn't need transportation. On top of that, the school had an excellent academic reputation.

I decided to join the industrial engineering program. I chose that because a friend told me that industrial engineers were in high demand. That's it. I wasn't passionate about the subject, but since I didn't mind math in high school and enjoyed electricity and chemistry, I thought it would be a good fit for me.

As a child, I'd dreamt of becoming a doctor like my uncle Francisco, my mother's brother. Francisco had graduated with a medical degree from the same public university I was now attending, but he moved to Brazil after graduation to complete his graduate program. Unfortunately, my dreams of becoming a doctor vanished when I realized that I didn't have the stomach to become one.

My high school friend's father was a doctor, and he took a small group of high school students to a local hospital for a job-shadowing experience. Things went well until a nurse asked me to help clean a patient's wound. I put on some gloves, walked to the patient's room with the nurse, and saw the injury. The next thing I remember is waking up on a hospital bed surrounded by other students. After I left the hospital that day, I promised myself I'd never return unless, of course, I needed medical attention.

Not long after this, I took a career aptitude test at school. Based on the results, it seemed that I was destined to be an attorney, a businessperson, or a priest. I had considered being a priest at one point, but I didn't feel that was my vocation. Instead, I thought I would become an attorney. I enjoyed reading about history and politics and thought I had a knack for arguing. However, this idea didn't last long, either. At one of my family's weekly visits to my paternal grandmother's home, I mentioned the idea of becoming a lawyer to her.

"A lawyer? Santiago, are you crazy?" she gasped.

"Why not? Don't they make a good living?" I countered.

"Yes, but only because they're all crooks. Do you want to be a crook?"

I didn't want to be a crook, so I decided not to follow my lawyerly dreams. Thus, when I applied to college, I picked a program based on what careers were in demand. Instead of finding my passion, I chose a career path that would make me somewhat employable after school.

*　　*　　*

At home, I would wake up early every day, make my bed, fold my clothes, and help our maid with breakfast. One of the first things I had noticed when I got back to Peru was that we had a maid. *Why do we have a maid at home?* I thought. This luxury no longer made sense to me. My father didn't live at home anymore, my mother didn't work, my brother Joaquin was at school for most of the day, and I could do things on my own.

It was nice to have the help, but I began to question why most middle-class families in Peru had a maid.

In fact, I began to question many things about my life in Peru. I started by thinking about my Peruvian high school, Colegio San José, or simply San José. This private Jesuit school was one of the best in the city, but it was years behind Mount Vernon High School in terms of technology. How could it be that San José had one computer lab with outdated computers, while Mount Vernon had three labs with modern computers? Why didn't San José provide Internet access for its students, while Mount Vernon had Internet in all its classrooms? At San José, all students have the same curriculum. At Mount Vernon, students chose their classes based on their interests. San José's library books seemed to collect dust. In my Iowa high school, the library was a popular and welcoming place. I received an excellent education at San José, and I made many lifelong friends there. However, I began to question whether that structured education had been the best thing for me.

Things weren't much different in college. My Peruvian university had outdated computer and science labs. Most of its professors were well respected academically, but the university appeared to have fewer resources than a modest community college in Iowa.

As time passed, I kept noticing more and more differences. Although this is part of the re-adaptation process for most returning exchange students, it seemed to be more than that for me. Before my trip to the United States, my world had been confined to a tiny bubble. Now, that bubble had burst. I began to wonder whether I wanted to continue my education in Peru.

Chapter Thirty-Nine
JOHNNY

June 2001

Weeks went by, and I settled into a comfortable routine. My father found a new job and was given a new company car. My mother was looking for a new job herself, but hadn't had any luck yet. My brother and I seemed to be accustomed to our family problems, so we went on with our lives. I spent most of my time either attending class or studying with Hugo, a high school friend who was in the same engineering program at my university. Hugo was smarter than I was when it came to math and physics. Chemistry was my forte though, so together we made quite a team. Hugo also played the guitar, so our study sessions often turned into jam sessions. We considered ourselves rebels because we listened to and played the music of Sui Generis, a famous Argentinean protest rock band from the 1970s.

By June, Hugo and I were busy preparing for our midterms. At my university, students had two testing periods: midterms and finals. Each test accounted for about forty-five percent of the class's final grade, with the remaining ten percent coming from participation or lab work. The grading scale for each test ran from zero to twenty, with eleven being the passing grade. A ten was the equivalent of a D. Our goal was to have an average grade of sixteen or more at the end of the semester.

We took all our tests in one week. First there was calculus, then physics, chemistry, and a technology class at the end. After every exam, Hugo and I got together to go over each question on the test. Although we thought all the tests were difficult, we were confident that we had done well.

A week after our tests, the results were posted in the lobby of the School of Engineering. Each student was given an identification number at the beginning of the year, and our test scores appeared next to our ID number. The first published scores were in physics.

Hugo got to the lobby first that morning, so he found his score before I did. When I saw him, he was wearing a huge grin. He'd gotten a seventeen, a high score. When he told me this, I was relieved. I had been worried about the results, because the midterms represented a high percentage of our final grade.

I looked at the list and found my ID number. Then I glanced at my score and felt my breath rush out of my body. I started to sweat, and a cold sensation crept down my spine. I checked the score again before walking away. I had gotten a three.

Seeing my shaken expression, Hugo asked, "Are you okay?"

"No, there has to be a mistake," I responded absently. I was trying to figure out what had happened. Hugo and I had compared our answers after every test. We hadn't been too far off from each other, and he had gotten a seventeen, so my getting a three made absolutely no sense.

"Why? What did you get?" he asked.

"A three."

Hugo smiled nervously, waiting for me to say I was joking.

"I need to talk to Professor Medina. I need to see my test," I told Hugo and hurried off to our professor's office.

When I got there, I knocked on the professor's semi-open door. "Professor Medina? Can I come in?" I asked.

"Come in," he said without taking his eyes away from some papers scattered across his desk. As I walked in, he raised his head and looked me up and down. "What can I do for you?"

"I just saw my score for the physics test, and I'd like to know if you could show me my test. I need to see what I did wrong," I said. At this point, I was noticeably nervous and sweating profusely. With a score of three on the midterm, my hopes of passing the class were almost nonexistent.

"What's your student number?" he asked. He was very dismissive, making me feel as if I were wasting his time.

"783562."

"Your name is Santiago, right?"

"Yes, sir," I said, surprised that he knew my name. Our physics class was a large lecture. Students could ask questions, but the professor rarely called on students to participate.

"Yes, I remember. Didn't you go to the United States last year?" I couldn't believe he remembered that fact, as we had a lot of students in our class. During our first class of the semester, he had asked us to share something interesting about ourselves, and I had said that I'd just returned from a trip to the United States.

"Yes sir, why?"

"I hear it's beautiful there," he said simply. He grabbed his briefcase, pulled out a bunch of papers, and went through them one by one. I could tell they were our tests. "No, sorry. I don't know what happened to yours. I know I had it at some point, but I don't know where it is now." This seemed strange. First, he mentioned my trip to the United States, and now he claimed to not know where my exam was.

"That can't be. I need to see it. I got a three. Who gets a three?"

"Well, it looks like you did," he said as he put all the tests back in his briefcase.

"Professor, look, I won't be able to pass the class with a three. I have all of my notes here. I studied. I need to see my test. There has to be a mistake," I said as I desperately placed my notes on his desk.

"I'm sorry, but there's nothing I can do."

"There has to be something you can do. Perhaps I can complete an extra project for extra points?" I asked. I was getting desperate, and he could tell. He could probably smell the fear and anxiety coursing through my veins.

He looked me straight in the eye for a brief moment and said, "I like Johnny Walker."

"I'm sorry?" I asked, surprised and confused.

"Or its equivalent," he added.

I couldn't believe it. One of my college professors had just asked for a bribe, requesting that I bring him a bottle of Johnny Walker or its cash equivalent. Based on this request, and the fact that he claimed not to have my test, I could only assume that he'd given me a low score on purpose so I'd be forced to bribe him.

"What?" I asked, disgusted by what I'd just heard.

"You know what to do. Now leave. I have nothing else to say."

An overwhelming feeling of anger washed over me. I had just spent several weeks studying for this test, only to find a professor asking for a bribe and pretending it was all part of the process. I was upset, frustrated, disgusted, and more than anything, disappointed.

I took a deep breath, picked up my papers, and turned to walk away without saying another word. But then, when I reached the door, I stopped, turned around, rapidly walked back over to the professor's desk, and threw all my papers in his face. I unloaded all of my frustrations on him and said many things that are not worth repeating.

Then I marched out of his office and straight to the head of the engineering department. After I waited outside of her office for a few minutes, she invited me in. I introduced myself and told her that I needed to speak to her about something important that had just occurred. She asked me to have a seat, and I told her exactly what had happened. She listened carefully and took notes. Then, without warning, she stopped me. "This is a grave accusation. Do you have any witnesses?"

"No, I don't."

"You know, without witnesses, this is going to be a case of your word against his, and I can tell you that he'll probably have the upper hand."

I shook my head and stared at the floor for a moment. "Thank you for your time," I said simply, got up, and walked away.

I ran into Hugo down in the lobby. He was discussing weekend plans with some of our other friends. "We need to talk," I said.

"What's up? Did you talk to Medina?" he asked.

I told him what had happened with the professor and the head of the department. I felt humiliated and needed to know if any other students had been forced to provide a bribe to this professor. Maybe we could go to the department head as a group to make a case against him.

Together, we asked around among the older students, and several said that this professor was known for doing such things, especially to students who appeared to have money. Maybe that's why he remembered that I had gone to the United States. He probably thought I came from a wealthy family, as many Peruvians usually associated a person's ability to visit the United States with being affluent. When I asked if any of them would be willing to come talk to the department head with me about this though, none of them were willing. They said that trying to reason with this professor was a lost cause. "Just pay up and move on," one of them advised. At that, the conversation moved on to a different topic, as though my problem were insignificant.

Hugo and I went to get some lunch and talk the matter over. We knew that most professors were honest, but as in most places, bad apples would turn up once in a while. The problem was that because of this bad apple, I was going to waste a semester, if not a year. Some other friends soon joined us, and the conversation turned to an upcoming soccer game for our engineering team. However, I couldn't stop thinking about that horrible moment when my professor asked me for a bribe. I couldn't stomach the fact that in order to pass this class, I would likely have to "pay up."

A couple of hours later, as I walked out of the building with Hugo, I told him that I would be leaving the university. He laughed and asked me to at least think about it for a few days. "You're too upset right now to make a rational decision," he argued.

"No, it's over. I'm not coming back anymore," I said with finality. True to my word, I never set foot in that place again.

Chapter Forty
DECISIONS

June 2001

When I got home that day, my dog, Cooper, welcomed me by jumping on me. He had been trained not to jump on people, but I think he sensed that I'd had a difficult day. I gave Cooper a big hug and grabbed his leash. I needed to clear my head, so we went for a walk.

As I walked around the neighborhood, I thought about what had happened that morning. I was disgusted, upset, and felt defeated. To make matters worse, as I listened to the local radio on my Walkman, I learned that my college professors had just announced their plans to go on an "indefinite" strike in thirty days. They had gone on strikes asking for higher pay before. This time, they were complaining about some of the interim president's policies. The bottom line was that since this was a public university, professors had the right to do this whenever they felt like it. The problem with these strikes was that they rarely worked. The professors might get the government's attention, but they didn't usually get what they asked for. In the meantime, thousands of students had to put their educations on hold.

I could go back to school the next day and pretend nothing had happened. I could walk into Professor Medina's office, beg for forgiveness, and give him a bottle of Johnny Walker. I could spend the next few years praying that our professors wouldn't go on strike for too long so I wouldn't lose a semester or a year of school. But did I want to do that? I wasn't sure that I did.

It was a warm and sunny day in Arequipa, and Cooper, my furry white Samoyed, didn't tolerate the heat well, so we had to keep our walk short. As soon as we got home, he ran to the garden to drink some water. I stood next to him until he finished. Then I poured some water into a glass for myself and walked up the stairs all the way to the roof of our house. Cooper followed me. Occasionally, when I needed to think about something, I would go up there. From the roof, I had a privileged view of the city. I could see El Misti, the iconic volcano, to the north and the entire city to the west. My home was secluded from the loud, chaotic Arequipa traffic, so it was quiet and peaceful. I could, however, see my university.

I sat on the roof with Cooper for about an hour. I thought about my future and began to get anxious. I didn't know what I was going to do next. All I knew was that I couldn't go back to that school. My time there was over. I needed a way out, but where? How? I could go to Lima, but how would I pay for school there? Even if I could pay for it, I would likely have to wait for a few months before I could apply to a school there. And what if I didn't get in?

I was lost.

"Cooper, I have to do something," I said to my dog. He looked up at me with his sweet face and licked my hand. I want to believe that he understood what I said. I stared out at my hometown for a few more minutes. "Alright buddy, it's time to go," I said and walked Cooper down to the backyard.

I went into my bedroom and found a box on my bed. It was full of pictures, all of them from my time in Iowa. My mother had gone to the store to develop my film from my trip and had left the box on my bed. I went through the pictures one-by-one and wrote the date and the location on the back of each photo. I couldn't stop smiling as I looked at them. I found pictures of my first time seeing snow, my high school friends, the soccer team, my host families, the Novaks' farm, my awkward prom experience, my trip to West Point, and my weeks in New York City.

I grabbed a picture of Kenneth and Linda and stared at it for some time. I thought of the first day we met, the day Kenneth took me hunting for the first time, and the day he had talked to me about going to school in the United States. Most importantly, I remembered what Linda had written on my card the day I left Iowa: "Iowa will always be your home."

I suddenly realized that my year in the United States hadn't merely been a learning experience; it had been a stepping-stone. That year in Iowa had opened my mind to new experiences and a new world. Those twelve months in Mount Vernon changed the way I saw the world.

I jumped off my bed and opened a box full of papers from my time in Iowa. I was looking for a specific document: my TOEFL test score. I went through every piece of paper until I found it. Then I grabbed my keys, a pen, a notebook, my wallet, and the document and ran to the closest Internet café. Most Peruvian families still didn't have an Internet connection in their home at the time, so we frequented these Internet "hubs" when we needed to get online.

I gave the café attendant enough money for three hours of Internet access and started researching Iowa universities. I started with Drake University, the University of Iowa, and Iowa State University. I researched their costs, possible scholarships, and TOEFL score requirements. All of these schools were out of my reach, financially. Even if I could obtain a scholarship, the costs were prohibitive unless I received a full ride.

I changed my strategy and started looking for schools that might offer me soccer scholarships. From the ones I found, I highlighted two: Drake University and North Iowa Area Community College, or NIACC. I emailed both soccer coaches. I never heard back from the Drake soccer coach, but I received an email from the NIACC soccer coach thirty minutes after I sent him my message. He had followed my high school career in Iowa and was interested in me. He sent me a few links and put me in contact with the international students' office. He explained that NIACC was a two-year school and for most students, it was a stepping-stone. After finishing their program at NIACC, most transferred to a four-year school.

I looked at the costs of attending NIACC, but this community college was still too expensive for me. Since I wasn't a United States citizen or resident, I had no access to student loans. However, it was the most affordable option, so I researched more scholarships. I wrote down the costs, the scholarship and academic programs, and read about the process of becoming an international student in the United States.

When my time was up at the Internet café, I hurried home and grabbed all the coins I had available. Ever since I was a child, my parents had taught me that if you want to make things happen, you need to make a sincere personal connection with others. Specifically, they taught me that a personal visit or phone call was much more effective than sending emails. So even though it would be expensive, I needed to call the school directly.

I ran to the closest phone booth and called the soccer coach. He answered. He seemed pleasantly surprised to receive my call and talked to me about the program. I liked what I heard and next called the international students' office. I spoke with a lovely lady who was also pleasantly surprised to receive my call and who provided me with additional information. I later learned that those phone calls made a difference. I had made a personal connection with them, and they became my advocates.

After speaking with the coach and the international students' office, I went back home, went into my room, and closed the door. I spent hours thinking about how I could make this work. I had gotten a high score on the TOEFL test, I was familiar with the Iowa culture, I had made meaningful connections there, and I had the school's soccer coach actively wanting me to attend that school. I had researched the school online, and it had a beautiful campus, a nice library, and a good computer lab. If nothing else, it had more computers than my Peruvian university did.

After pondering for a few hours, I made the decision that changed my life forever: I would go back to Iowa and attend college there. Only one question remained: how in the world was I going to afford it?

Chapter Forty-One
IOWA-BOUND

June to mid-August 2001

In the following days, I developed a strategy. I figured that if I could just find the funds to attend NIACC for the first year, once there, I'd be able to find a way to pay for my second year. Before going anywhere though, I needed to talk with my parents. I needed their buy-in, but most importantly, I needed their financial help.

"Mom, I've made a decision," I said one night during dinner. I hadn't told my mother about the issues I'd had with my college professor, so she had no idea I'd needed to make any kind of decision about my future. Luckily for me, the college professors had moved their strike up a few weeks, and since the university was closed during their protests, she thought I wasn't attending class because of the strike.

"What kind of decision are you talking about?" she asked, surprised.

"I can't go back to school here," I said.

She had a puzzled look on her face, which turned into one of her classic, terrifying looks. She already had big eyes, and in that moment, they opened more than I had ever seen before. "And what do you propose to do with your life?" she asked, noticeably worried about my statement.

"I'm going back to Iowa."

"What? Why?" It definitely wasn't the answer she was expecting.

"College."

She seemed to want to burst out laughing, but managed to contain herself. She looked at me for a moment before saying, "Santiago, we can't afford to send you to school there."

"I know. I just need some help to get me there. I'll figure it out once I'm in Iowa."

At that time, my parents were in the process of selling our home as part of their separation of assets, so I suggested that they could direct some of the proceeds to my education. Apparently, that seemed reasonable enough, because my parents discussed it and agreed.

In the meantime, I needed to find a sponsor. In order to attend school in the United States, international students need to present a sponsor to their school of choice. This sponsor needs to be able to ensure that the student will have sufficient financial means to attend school. My parents were going to help me with the first year, but I needed to prove to NIACC that I had someone with the financial means to sponsor me for two years. I asked the only person I could at the time: my uncle Francisco. He lived in Brazil, but was visiting my family for a few weeks. He was not only my godfather, but the only person in my family who had the financial means to become a sponsor. We had a long conversation about my plan, and he agreed to sponsor me, but he made it clear that—due to Brazil's financial instability—he couldn't guarantee any real help if things changed for him there. "And things could change quickly," he added. It was worth the risk for me. And just like that, I had a sponsor.

Fortunately, we found a buyer for our house quickly. My parents bought separate condos, paid some debts, and managed their money as they thought best. After everything was said and done, there was seven thousand dollars left for me. For my family, that was a lot of money.

I continued my research and learned that international students, under a student visa, could work up to twenty hours per week on campus. I did the math and realized that if I could find a job at the school, I would have enough money to pay for my first year.

In just forty-five days, I had received my admission package from NIACC, discussed my plan with my parents, convinced Francisco to be my sponsor, and received seven thousand dollars from my parents. I was going to make this work.

I completed the forms as quickly as I could, gathered all the financial information I needed, and submitted the admission package online. Within a week, the school accepted me, and I received an I-20 form—the form I needed to take to the United States Embassy to obtain my student visa. I applied for a visa, and received it in a matter of days. As soon as I had that, I purchased my plane ticket to Iowa and began to plan my departure. Everything was happening so quickly. In a matter of sixty days, I had gone from leaving my Peruvian university to preparing to leave my country once again.

After purchasing my plane ticket, I was left with about $5800 in my bank account. I still had enough to pay for my first semester and part of my second semester in Iowa, so I wasn't too worried yet. Besides, I still hadn't received a response from all the scholarship programs I'd applied to, and I was hoping to get additional assistance from the soccer program. Sure enough, just a few days after I purchased my plane ticket, I received good news from my soccer coach: the school was prepared to give me a scholarship of four hundred dollars per semester so I could play soccer for them. I would be leaving Peru the first week of August, just in time to join the soccer team for pre-season training.

Things were going well until the Monday night three weeks before my departure, when I felt an intense pain in my back. It was so terrible that I couldn't move, and my mother had to take me to the hospital. After some tests, the doctor said that I needed to have emergency surgery. This surgery required that I stay in the hospital for a couple of nights.

After the successful operation, I asked my doctor when I could start playing soccer again. He said that it would be a couple of months before I could even start jogging again.

A couple of months? Now what? I thought. *What will happen to my scholarship?* It wasn't a significant amount of money for most, but it was significant to me.

"Santiago, you need to be careful. Your health is not a game," the doctor reminded me repeatedly in front of my parents.

"I understand. I'll do what you tell me to do," I said.

A week later, I started to feel better and could stand up again, but walking was still difficult. My trip was still two weeks away, so I continued my preparations. I read my grammar books, hoping to perfect my English as much as possible before going to college. I had the money to attend school for the first semester, and even if they took away my scholarship because I couldn't play soccer, I was confident that I would find a way to pay for the second.

One week before my departure, we received my hospital bill. My parents couldn't afford to pay for it, so I had to use part of my small college fund to cover the cost.

I panicked. After paying for my hospital bill, I only had three thousand dollars left. Even if I worked twenty hours per week on campus from day one, which was unlikely to happen, I would barely have enough money to pay for the first semester of school.

"Santiago, what are you going to do?" my mother asked as we discussed my finances. She didn't have the money to help me out any further, and neither did my father. Francisco said that he couldn't help me at the moment. I was in trouble, and I hadn't even left Peru yet.

"Don't worry, Mom. I'll figure it out. I always do," I assured her, hoping to ease her anxiety. In reality, I didn't know how I was going to make it work anymore.

Within a few days, I found myself back at the Lima International Airport, on my way to the United States. I limped through the airport, as I still couldn't walk well, until I found my gate. I nervously waited to board the plane.

Once on the plane, I shed a few tears as the pilot prepared for lift-off. I was overwhelmed with emotions. I was sad to be leaving my family and friends again, but excited about this new adventure. I was also deeply worried about moving to the United States for college with a rather small college fund. *People have done a lot with much less*, I told myself. I didn't know what I was about to face, but I knew I would figure something out.

I always did.

ABOUT THE AUTHOR

Pedro A. Salazar is an attorney and writer. He grew up in Arequipa, Peru. After living in Iowa as a high school exchange student, he decided to move to the United States to attend college. He graduated from Wartburg College, in Waverly, Iowa, with a BA in business administration and political science. He earned an MBA and a J.D. from Drake University in Des Moines, Iowa. Pedro lives in Charlotte, North Carolina, with his wife.

Made in the USA
Monee, IL
30 January 2020

21058966R00171